What People Are Saying About

DITCH THAT TEXTBOOK

"Want to engage and inspire the new or veteran 21st century teacher? This is the book to get them. Want to renew your own commitment to thriving in teaching, not just surviving? This is the book to get yourself. *Ditch That Textbook* is a well-executed, high beam dismount from inert teaching. With Miller as coach, we not only 'stick the landing,' we grow wings."

—**RICK WORMELI**, Assessment and Middle-Level Instruction Expert and Author, *Fair Isn't Always Equal* (@rickwormeli2)

"*Ditch That Textbook* is filled with real-world advice for teachers looking to make their courses relevant for today's student. The book is more about infusing your teaching with the same skills that we want from our students. Creativity, problem solving, and use of technology as a tool to improve learning are all at the heart of this text."

—**JEFF CHARBONNEAU**, 2013 National Teacher of the Year (@JeffCharbonneau)

"We are living and learning in incredible times. The pace at which information is changing is rapidly increasing each day. Teachers can no longer rely on the static information printed in books as the sole source in the classroom. In *Ditch That Textbook*, Matt offers some very practical ideas for making the most of digital resources that can truly expose students to a wide world of learning."

—**STEVEN W. ANDERSON**, Learning Evangelist and #EdChat Co-founder (@web20classroom)

"Classroom teachers are in constant competition with the digital world to capture and maintain their students' attention. In *Ditch That Textbook*, Matt Miller provides you with a roadmap to ensure your teaching is engaging, motivating and relevant for today's 21st century learners. His easy-to-implement and fresh approach to re-designing curriculum will help you create a classroom where students run to get IN rather than out."

—**DAVE AND SHELLEY BURGESS**, Dave Burgess Consulting and Author, *Teach Like a PIRATE* (@burgessdave @burgess_shelley)

"Matt Miller's *Ditch That Textbook* is a book that delivers sound advice, relatable anecdotes, and an actionable roadmap for educators to embrace progressive thinking about education and infuse technology to upgrade their classroom practice in the name of learning. This book is perfect for any teacher who is looking for inspiration and ideas to move beyond the traditional model of educator in order to make teaching more engaging and learning more impactful."

—**Adam Bellow**, eduTecher Founder and 2011 ISTE Outstanding Young Educator of the Year (@adambellow)

"With *Ditch That Textbook*, Matt Miller does an exceptional job at sharing his story and how each of us has the ability and responsibility to stop doing things the way we've 'always done them.' Matt shares practical advice and great tools. This book should be on every educator and education leader's must-read list."

—**TODD NESLONEY**, 2014 Bammy Awards National Elementary Teacher of the Year (@TechNinjaTodd)

"The title of this book might sound alarming, but ditching the textbook is exactly what needs to be done. In an age where many schools are still training students to work in a factory, Matt Miller moves past sweeping rhetoric and shows teachers how to move their classes into the future. This is a quick, energetic read that will leave you inspired to take the next step in your classroom!"

—**DON WETTRICK**, Innovation Specialist and
Author, *Pure Genius* (@DonWettrick)

"Like it or not, the heyday of textbook-style learning is essentially over. In the absence of the traditional path, educators at all levels need a new path, a new workflow, a new mindset. *Ditch That Textbook* provides the most developed process for moving from a textbook dominated pedagogy that I've seen thus far. Bravo!"

—**JON CORIPPO**, CUE Rock Star Teacher Camps Founder (@jcorippo)

"Integrating technology is tough, but *Ditch That Textbook* aims to make this journey more meaningful for teachers and students! This book is filled with fun ideas and inspiring examples from a teacher who once lectured students quite a bit. You'll enjoy Matt Miller's authentic voice as he shares some of his favorite tips and resources for getting your students to enjoy learning again."

—**SHELLY SANCHEZ TERRELL**, #EdChat Co-Founder and
Author, *The 30 Goals Challenge for Teachers* (@ShellTerrell)

"Preparing students for the future can be a daunting task for educators. As teachers, we must help our students to become lifelong learners in a world that is constantly being reinvented by new technology and innovations. In *Ditch That Textbook*, Matt Miller addresses these issues and gives teachers practical steps to transform their classrooms. Matt brings a refreshing approach to digital learning that any teacher can follow. For teachers looking to find new ways to empower their students and prepare them for the future, this book is a must!"

—**Kasey Bell**, Award-Winning Digital Learning Consultant and Blogger (@ShakeUpLearning)

"*Ditch That Textbook* is a collection of ideas, considerations, and suggestions that will help teachers re-examine their purpose in today's educational climate. With honest stories and a familiar voice, Matt Miller skillfully describes changes teachers can make in their classroom that will help them adapt to today's educational landscape, and presents compelling arguments to get teachers to DITCH their old ways of thinking!"

—**Paul Solarz**, Author, *Learn Like a PIRATE* (@PaulSolarz)

DITCH
THAT
TEXTBOOK

FREE
YOUR TEACHING AND
REVOLUTIONIZE
YOUR CLASSROOM

Matt
Miller

Published by Dave Burgess Consulting, Inc.
San Diego, CA
http://daveburgessconsulting.com

Edited by Erin K. Casey
Cover Design by Genesis Kohler
Interior Design by My Writers' Connection

Library of Congress Control Number: 2015937029
Paperback: ISBN: 978-0-9861554-0-6
Ebook: ISBN: 978-0-9861554-1-3

First Printing: April 2015

To Melanie, whose love and companionship have encouraged everything I've attempted since I met her;

To Mom and Dad, who crafted the person I've become through constant support and guidance;

To Cassie, Hallie, and Joel, who never cease to make me smile and love life more.

I'm grateful to a couple of pirates who took a chance on me, bringing me aboard their ship to help me accomplish a lifelong dream. Thanks, Dave and Shelley.

"In the same way, let your light shine before others, that they may see your good deeds and glorify your Father in heaven."
—Matthew 5:16 NIV

Contents

Pitch That Textbook

Pitch That Curriculum

DITCH THAT TEXTBOOK

INTRODUCTION

I had never seen students run for the door so fast.

When the bell rang that day in 2007, it might as well have been a fire alarm. It was like the kids had springs in their seats.

We had just completed forty-eight minutes of fascinating lecture and practice questions from a high school Spanish textbook. (Fascinating might be a bit of a stretch.) The students weren't engaged or paying attention, so I punished them with extra work to be completed silently in their seats.

The truth is, teaching through lectures and textbook exercises bored me as much as it did them. I hated the idea of being the guy whose goal was teaching from Page One to the end of the textbook every year. (Actually, I wasn't even that guy, because we only made it halfway through the book in a school year.) I knew there had to be a better way to teach.

I wanted my classes to be different.

I wanted my classroom to be a place where great learning experiences happened.

I wanted my students to talk in Spanish all the time and to learn by doing.

Half-baked grammar exercises from a textbook weren't going to accomplish those goals, much less produce lifelong language speakers.

Anyone who's been in education very long knows its practices are deep-seated and slow to evolve. Many aren't best practices; some aren't even close. That day in 2007, I realized my classes had to change. I was sick of teaching by the textbook. I wanted something better—for my students and for me.

Early in my career, I thought I understood teaching. A bit of a follower at the time, I expected to do what I had experienced as a student myself and what my peers did in their classrooms. I expected my textbook to be the curriculum for my class. In my paradigm of education, we read the textbook and used lots of worksheets, workbooks, and multiple-choice tests. And sure, those methods were easy enough to use, but as time went on, I realized education could be so much more engaging and interesting.

Since you picked up this book, I'm assuming you may feel a lot like I did: trapped and burned out on traditional textbook teaching. You know the potential exists for innovative, engaging, and revolutionary education. With the right ideas, right tools, and right people, all put in the right order, you're sure something amazing could happen in your classroom. If that sounds like you, then you're ready to ditch your textbooks.

Ditch That Textbook isn't necessarily about tossing a stack of hardback textbooks out a three-story window, hearing a satisfying thump on the ground, and brushing the dust off your hands. (But if that's what you think you need to do, make sure you get it on video!) In fact, if your school requires you to teach from a certain textbook, the last thing you should do is defy that mandate. That's not what I'm suggesting. No, this book is about evolving and finding better ways to teach.

In the *Oxford Pocket Dictionary of Current English*, you'll find "textbook" as a noun: "a book used as a standard work for the study of a particular subject." You'll also find it as an adjective: "conforming to or corresponding to a standard or type that is prescribed or widely held by theorists."

For me, the standard that was "widely held by theorists" just wasn't working. So I decided to toss out the old standard and look for a new, more effective approach to teaching. Along the way, DITCH became my model for deciding what and how to teach:

DIFFERENT: Using teaching methods that differ from what students see day after day, class after class.

INNOVATIVE: Inventing new ideas or modifying others' ideas, then testing them in the classroom, even if their success isn't guaranteed.

TECH-LADEN: Incorporating digital sites, tools, and devices to learn more efficiently or in new and different ways.

CREATIVE: Tapping into students' original ideas as well as creating and producing meaningful work. (After all, creative has the word create in it!)

HANDS-ON: Letting students make and try things on their own.

In the coming chapters, I'll show you how using the DITCH model can help you free your teaching and revolutionize your classroom. Before we get started, here's a brief overview of what we'll cover in *Ditch That Textbook*.

Why Go Digital? First things, first. If a textbook isn't going to be your primary resource, what is? Here's a hint: Your students are already using it. Technology, specifically Internet apps and websites, can be a powerful tool for you and your students. If you're uncertain about how or why to join the digital revolution, I hope you'll find this first section insightful and encouraging. Once we've reviewed the benefits and practicalities of going digital, we'll look at ways technology can help you can improve your class as you ditch outdated mindsets, methods, and plans.

Ditch that Mindset: Textbook ideas about education lead to stagnant (aka boring) teaching. Teachers' entrenched mindsets often become the lore of former students who tell and retell stories of mindless classes or nonsensical practices. None of us wants to be the source of these stories. And yet, even when we know a method isn't working, we can feel powerless to make a change. It's in those moments that we must ditch our textbook ideas and blaze new trails, going boldly where no teacher has gone before. It's even okay to settle for where we have never gone before; just get out of those mental ruts!

Ditch that Textbook: Textbook ditching is about throwing out meaningless, pedestrian teaching and learning practices. It's about examining what we do in our classrooms, determining whether it gets the results we need, and taking action. That could mean completely discarding what we did previously or simply rewiring the circuitry of a lesson with plenty of potential. It could also mean reflecting on what is working, smiling and saying, "Yeah, that did the trick."

Ditch that Curriculum: For me, to fully ditch my most ineffective teaching styles, I had to ditch my curriculum, too. That was pretty easy because I had no curriculum when I started teaching! I pulled together all of my best teaching ideas, the main lessons I wanted to include in my classes, and the activities that could help make it all happen. I found research and best practices to support my ideas and followed academic standards and school policies. Then, I crafted my courses using the DITCH model as my standard.

The result is a curriculum that engages my students and makes learning fun.

Simply put, in *Ditch That Textbook* you'll discover why and how to change your mindset and methods so you can create great learning experiences for your students. And don't think the irony of the *Ditch That Textbook* guy writing a book is lost on me. For most of us educators, reading is probably still our favorite way to learn.

This book isn't a step-by-step instruction manual for how to teach without textbooks. I'm not sure that book should ever be written. Legislation and school/district policies already intrude too much into teachers' creative processes; you don't need another rule to follow or standard to meet. Instead, *Ditch That Textbook* is designed to be a support system, toolbox, and manifesto. It's a collection of ideas, considerations, and suggestions to help you free yourself as an educator to create the classroom and the teaching style that you want.

Let's get started!

SECTION 1

WHY GO DIGITAL?

Digital technology has changed the game in education. The devices students carry in their pockets are supremely more powerful than the massive computers that helped put a man on the moon in 1969. The Internet makes it possible to communicate with virtually anyone around the world in a matter of seconds instead of weeks or months.

Today's advanced technology offers many advantages; it also presents a new set of challenges. If harnessed correctly, technology can help classrooms transform into places where students learn valuable, relevant lessons that will help equip them for their future lives and careers. If technology is misused or, worse, omitted from the classroom, students will miss out on opportunities to develop important skills they'll need to keep up with a constantly changing marketplace. If our job is to prepare students for the real world, the question isn't *if* we should go digital, but *how* to go digital—starting now.

‹Chapter 1›
FREE ACCESS

Let's imagine, for a moment that I—a humble teacher and blogger from Indiana—wanted to meet with John Dewey. I'm talking about *John Dewey*, the groundbreaking educational thinker and reformer from the 1900s. We both have had a passion for connecting education to the interests and experiences of students, so I tend to think we would have a great conversation. We might not become BFFs, but perhaps productive professional acquaintances. (I know, I know, it's a stretch on reality. Humor me.)

To meet with Dewey—a single encounter, maybe over dinner—I would need to travel to his location. He was on the faculty of the University of Chicago until 1904. Since I'm from Indiana, a trip to Chicago would be much shorter than going to New York, where he spent the majority of the rest of his life.

In 1904, even a short trip would have required a lot of planning. There's a good chance a train would have made the trip from somewhere nearby in Indiana to Chicago, but getting to the train station from my home would take at least a day's travel. Purchasing a train ticket on a teacher's salary would be no easy feat, but let's give me the benefit of the doubt that I could pay for the fare. The trip to Chicago, at top speeds of maybe fifty miles per hour, would take the better part of the day. Once there, I'd have to get on Dewey's schedule. He was certainly in high demand and very busy so it could easily be a few days before we could sit down together, which would add room and board to my travel expenses. Then, it would take two days to get back home.

You can see how, with no cell phones, no email, no virtual assistants, or valet horse-parking services, getting access to great minds would have been quite difficult and costly back in the early 1900s. My single visit with Mr. Dewey would be next to impossible without forsaking my livelihood and financial stability.

The Perks of Living in a Connected World

Circumstances have certainly changed in the last century. When I think of the inspiring people out there now with whom I would love to have dinner, Rick Wormeli comes to mind. He's an advocate of standards-based grading and a very active Twitter user. He may not be the next coming of John Dewey, but he's a pretty bright guy who has significantly expanded my thinking about education.

Rick lives in Virginia and travels all over the world to speak about education. But to meet with me, he wouldn't even need to leave his living room. On the spur of the moment, he and I could set up a Google Hangout video chat to discuss ideas for changing my outdated grading practices in my Spanish classes. If he was too busy to meet me via Google Hangout, I could catch him on Twitter, possibly during the #sblchat chat on Wednesdays between 9 and 10 p.m. Eastern time. If I had a pointed question and could articulate it in one hundred forty characters or less, he would probably shoot me a quick tweet. (He has in the past!)

These days, we can turn to technology if we want to swap ideas with colleagues, connect with a faraway friend, or see a famous landmark in another country. Through social media we can stay in touch with people all over the globe. With Facebook, I keep up with friends in Mexico City as easily as I do with my parents half an hour away! Video chats via Skype, FaceTime, and Google Hangouts all deliver the free "talking videophone"... one of my favorite futuristic features predicted by the movie *Back to the Future Part II*. Other communication apps, like Voxer and its walkie-talkie capability, help us connect faster and more easily than ever before. All you need is a smartphone, a computer, or a tablet, which many of us already have, and an Internet connection, something that's readily available to many people around the globe.

Technology provides unbridled access to our students as well. They can video chat with experts about the topics they're studying and talk face-to-face with the authors of books they're reading. Video chats make places even more accessible as many facilities schedule free educational tours and demonstrations. For example, Greater Clark County Schools, a district in Southern Indiana near Louisville, Kentucky, treated students in all of its schools

Technology provides unbridled access to our students.

to an end-of-the-year, behind-the-scenes video tour of Churchill Downs. All it took was some scheduling by the school district.

In my own classroom, students leveraged this transformational technology to engage in a virtual cultural exchange with a class of English language learners in Valencia, Spain. What a huge, game-changing opportunity for my kids! Most of them have not traveled outside the United States, and many of them never will, and yet they have had the rich experience of talking with people from a different country and culture.

These previously impossible connections can revolutionize education—if teachers are willing to give them a shot. At conferences and across the blogosphere, I've seen countless references to collaborative tools and technology's potential to bridge the miles between people and places. What I haven't seen are many real-life examples of classes leveraging these tech tools. Why the lack of implementation? It's not that the technology is brand new; social media, video chats, shared documents and the like have been around for years.

What's missing, I believe, are the vision for the power of these new techniques and digital resources and the willingness to risk trying them. Instead of testing a new idea or tool, "paralysis by analysis" takes hold. We overanalyze new options, mull over all of the things we don't know, think about how students will react, and then we don't act! Let me challenge you to catch the vision and take the first step. Jump in, even if you don't know exactly how it will turn out! Don't let transformative and innovative learning ideas get left in your planning notebook where they won't do you or your students any good.

<Chapter 2>
BOOST YOUR EFFICIENCY

I ran across a picture on Facebook the other day of Austin Powers, "International Man of Mystery" (played by Mike Myers). He was leaning toward the camera with a half smile on his face. The caption read: "Waiting until the morning to make photocopies for class? I, too, like to live dangerously."

That is living dangerously, isn't it? Sometimes you can walk right into the workroom with nobody in sight and churn out your copies in no time. But on the day you really need them, and need them *now*, a line wraps around the room. That's when I used to head to the front office to borrow the copier—a trick not all of the teachers at my school know—but sometimes that copier is claimed, too!

You can keep living dangerously and continue making photocopies. Or you could skip that drama and use technology to distribute all your files digitally. For me, that means creating documents, presentations, etc., with Google Apps and putting links to them on my class website. (I'll explain more about that in a later

> Going the digital route is worth it simply for the time and effort we can save.

chapter.) Even without the unique learning experiences technology offers, going the digital route is worth it simply for the time and effort we can save.

Sometimes, I think about what teaching would be like if I had begun my career twenty years earlier, back when the Apple IIGS computers were showing up in classrooms. Back then, I was still in elementary school, and we could play a handful of educational games (Math Blaster!) and create banners with Print Shop on those computers. Every couple of weeks we visited the computer lab. I can still remember barely holding in my excitement as our class walked in a single-file line toward that magical place. There, I played Oregon Trail, a favorite I still play online, and tried to survive the trek from Independence, Missouri, to the Willamette Valley in Oregon, in a Conestoga wagon. If all went well, my digital family made the journey without dying of dysentery. (I didn't know what dysentery was as a child, but I knew I didn't want it!)

With all the computers sequestered out of the daily reach of students and teachers, their impact on the day-to-day activities of planning and creating lessons was minimal, at least at my school. Hand-written lessons, photocopied worksheets, and long hours correcting assignments and recording grades consumed teachers' evenings and weekends.

My teaching experience has been completely different from that of my childhood teachers. Today's technology allows me to work smarter and faster so my focus can stay on creating quality learning opportunities for my students. It allows me to be more productive and efficient so I'm not at school all hours of the day. For example:

- BEFORE, taking a field trip could take weeks of planning and permission slip signing. A trip could take all day and would require coordination of chaperones, buses, and lunch. TODAY, we can create field trip experiences within a class period by participating in Skype video chats to virtually anywhere in the world.

- BEFORE, creating teaching materials required good penmanship, maybe a little art skill, and lots of patience. TODAY, I can generate basic activities with Google Forms and Documents in a matter of minutes, or students can generate these activities on their own.

- BEFORE, grading quizzes and tests required a red pen, a comfortable seat, and more than an hour of uninterrupted time. TODAY, simple assignments can be auto-graded with Google add-ons like Flubaroo. More complex assignments can be assessed and returned to students at any time of day, morning or night. As soon as you're finished with their files on the Web, students can access them immediately.

- BEFORE, finding a document to distribute to kids meant digging through filing cabinets, flipping through file folders, and finding the right document… assuming it got filed in the right place. TODAY, a quick keyword search through a database of digital documents can help you find a file in seconds.

- BEFORE, all the books in your cabinets and on your shelves could yield great ideas—if you could only remember and track down the right book. TODAY, a search engine can find those ideas for you quickly, or colleagues on social media can suggest other ideas within minutes.

Why go digital? In part, because it makes your life easier! If you're like me, you love to teach, but it's not your entire identity. I have a family I love—a wonderful wife and three great kids. I have friends to keep up with and extended family to visit. Places to go, people to see, things to do. Even though grading and planning are important parts of my job, I don't want them to consume my entire life. I'm so thankful I am teaching during this time in history in which technology allows me to get more done in less time. I know that you, too, have a lot of life to live outside of grading papers. Let's outsource and automate what we can with technology and spend our time doing what's most important: living life!

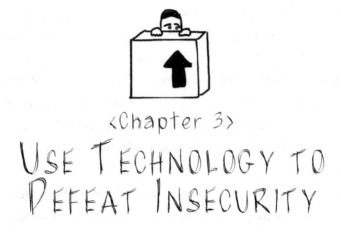

<Chapter 3>
USE TECHNOLOGY TO DEFEAT INSECURITY

Have you ever wanted a do-over with a student?
Have you ever wished for an opportunity to start fresh or take back something you've done or said? I have. For me, "Kay" is the student I wish I could turn back the clock for. She was in my Spanish and etymology classes, and let's just say, I learned a lot from her.

In some ways, Kay was like any standard, high-school, non-conformist (if the words "standard" and "non-conformist" can be used together). She dyed her hair and had a variety of piercings. She hung out with kids who dressed and looked just like her. But there was something different about Kay. She was quiet. Granted, if a friend really provoked Kay, she would deliver a verbal lashing with obscenities that would make a sailor blush. I got to accompany her to the principal's office after one such occasion. But for the most part, in the hallways, in the classroom, and at lunch, she wasn't chatty.

Kay kept her thoughts to herself, but I could see the gears turning in her mind. Unfortunately, at least in my classes, she didn't have an outlet to express herself. Kay didn't raise her hand to talk in class. She hated "rotating conversations," during which students asked and answered questions for a few minutes before changing partners. Speaking wasn't her thing. In fact, just before a group presentation in front of the class, she decided not to speak, even though she knew her decision could hurt her and her classmates' grades.

Kay is the student who comes to mind when I hear the phrase "still waters run deep." On the outside, she was like a calm, glassy lake, but there were gallons of ideas under the surface. And I really wanted to know what was going on beneath that quiet exterior.

Kay finally gave me a glimpse into her thoughts when we started doing backchannels in class. A backchannel is a separate, often text-based, discussion students engage in while they're receiving information via a lecture, a movie, a television show, or a PowerPoint presentation. Students use a digital device to participate in a behind-the-scenes chat so as not to disturb others trying to listen.

Backchannels provide the perfect outlet for students who have something to say but refuse to open up in class discussions. When everyone participates in the conversation, no one feels singled out. As a result, inhibitions about sharing decrease and the courage to speak up increases. Plus, when everyone types at once, the teacher spends less time calling on students one by one.

One day, instead of asking questions out loud, I turned to TodaysMeet.com, a very simple, easy-to-use backchannel. Students signed into our chat room by entering their names. In this online space, they could then engage in the discussion and ask and answer questions.

> Technology provides outlets
> that let even the shyest
> students feel comfortable
> enough to be themselves.

I had very little luck connecting with Kay in my Spanish classes. Breaking through the barrier of expressing oneself in a new language is challenging enough for the most uninhibited students. It ended up being too much of a challenge for Kay. But things were different in my etymology class.

We started a class conversation on a backchannel with the stipulation that all answers had to include words with the roots we were studying. To my surprise, as the questions flew and the discussion got interesting, Kay jumped right in the midst of it. She didn't have to speak out loud in front of everyone. She could answer without everyone looking at her. There she was, in the middle of the conversation, apparently very comfortable expressing her thoughts and opinions. I felt so proud of her and was fascinated to learn what was really going on in her mind.

Seeing Kay express herself so easily through the backchannel that day made me regret forcing her to participate in that group presentation. My motives were pure: I wanted to encourage her to overcome her fears and change her feelings about speaking in front of her peers. Instead, what I'd hoped would be a positive experience turned sour. I wish I would have given her more alternative opportunities to showcase her genius in my class.

I suppose we all have experiences—good and bad—that drive us as teachers. Our best course of action is to allow those "I wish I would have…" moments to motivate us to improve for the next round of students.

Just by being herself, Kay showed me a powerful reason for ditching those old textbook mentalities and going digital: defeating insecurity. Technology provides outlets that let even the shyest students feel comfortable enough to be themselves. Some kids are mortified at the thought of standing up and talking in front of all of those people, some of whom may not have been too kind to them in the past. Tech tools like TodaysMeet put a barrier between insecure students and the physical eyes and ears of the other students. They give voice to just the message. Students can write and create and record without having to see a whole classroom of eyes. That freedom is empowering to students like Kay, and it might make the difference between isolation and inclusion in the classroom.

Insecurity will always be uncomfortable. Our students will always have to deal with feelings of insecurity, at school and beyond. If we can do our part to help them manage and defeat it, we'll give them skills they'll use in real life.

<Chapter 4>

EMPOWER STUDENTS TO FIND THEIR PASSIONS

What if you enrolled in business school to earn your MBA, but instead of learning about business plans and profit and loss statements, the professors taught you everything you needed to know about farming? How equipped would you feel to manage a corporate office? Not very. Right? My bet is you'd feel frustrated about the time and effort you'd invested in an education that didn't suit your career choice.

Unfortunately, a similar scenario plays out in our schools every year. The skills and habits students learn in school directly contradict what their future employers want. Research from an MIT study shows the demand for routine work—think turning widgets in a factory—and manual labor have been on the decline since 1960. Today's employees are doing more non-routine, analytical, and interpersonal activities. In a nutshell: they're using their brains and their imaginations more than their muscles.[1]

Wait a second. *Routine work.* Doesn't that sound a lot like what students do in so many classrooms? Students everywhere are drowning in busywork: worksheets, workbook pages, and repetitive, simplistic activities.

For decades, students have been stuck in the "do what I'm told" mentality. Their thinking goes like this: "I'll go to school because that's what I'm told to do. When I get there, I'll go to class and listen to the teacher, because that's what I'm supposed to do. When the teacher stops teaching and gives me an assignment, that's exactly what I'll do because she told me to do it. If I keep doing what I'm told long enough and well enough, I'll graduate from school."

In a TED talk titled "Changing Education Paradigms," creativity expert Sir Ken Robinson talked about what happens to students as they get older and progress through the education system. In the talk, he noted, "They have spent ten years at school being told that there is one answer. It's at the back. And don't look. And don't copy, because that's cheating. I mean, outside schools, that's called 'collaboration'."[2]

What has this passive, routine-driven system produced? Generations of teenagers who reach the end of their compulsory schooling and have no idea who they are or what they should do next.

Students know how to play the "game of school." They can complete the activities, follow directions, choose the correct letter in multiple-choice tests, and get the grade. But then graduation puts an end to the game, and it's time to, as financial guru Dave Ramsey says, "go out and kill something and bring it back to the cave." They suddenly realize how ill-equipped they are for real life. They have no idea what motivates them, so rather than pursue a career with passion and purpose, they randomly send out resumes and get stuck in uninspiring jobs.

> You can open your students'
> minds to new possibilities
> and empower them to
> explore what drives them.

I know this because it happened to me. I was a good student. I graduated in the top ten percent of my class in high school and decided to study journalism in college. I was great at playing the game of school and continued playing it very well in college. I graduated as the top journalism student of the year and took a prestigious reporter internship right after graduation.

Right before I graduated, it dawned on me that *I had no idea what I wanted to write about.* I was about to leave college and go to work for a daily newspaper, and I didn't have a passion. I loved to write. I loved the atmosphere at newspapers, but I couldn't build a career writing about them!

With a minor in political science, I figured I should write about local politics. That plan crashed and burned as I quickly learned that covering county government, and even being a reporter, did not fit my personality and strengths. It wasn't until *after* I'd started a career as a reporter that I evaluated my passions and discovered that helping people was what I really wanted to do. I then realized I was built to be a teacher, not a newspaper reporter. A few visits to my wife's school—she teaches middle school social studies— confirmed my true calling. The rest is history. Unfortunately, it took a failed journalism career and additional college semesters to learn that lesson.

Expand Your Students' Worlds

When teachers determine to ditch their textbook mentalities, practices, and curricula, they often find it easier to help students discover what motives them. One way you can empower your students to free themselves from the limiting, "do what I'm told" mindset is to introduce digital tools that cater to their unique passions and interests—and there are so many resources out there. With a simple Web search, students can find pages and pages of information on topics that interest them. From instructional videos and photo galleries, to research and personal reflections in blog posts, students can access vast quantities of material in formats that suit their unique learning styles.

My brother-in-law exemplifies how the Internet can help students learn and improve, even outside the classroom. He's in eighth grade and is passionate about basketball. This kid is a great ball handler who can shoot a jump shot with either hand. Some of his talent is genetic and some is the result of many hours of practice. But he has also improved his skills through exhaustive online study. He has watched countless instructional videos, clips of pro basketball players' best moves, workout videos, and strength training guides. He has tapped into the resources at his disposal (which far exceed what I could have imagined when I was his age), and used them to become one of the best young basketball players in his area.

No one taught him how to develop a solid training regimen or plan a practice session for himself; he learned those things on his own through Internet research. He used his home computer as a tool to find the information he needed to become the kind of basketball player he wanted to be. Then, he took action. He engaged in training programs. He went outside and practiced ball-handling drills. He adjusted his release until the shot felt just right. All those factors—skill, passion, access to information, practice, and determination—contributed to his success.

When you use the Internet and online tools to expand the scope of your class, you can open your students' minds to new possibilities and empower them to explore what drives them. Would exposure to information like that have helped me find my purpose sooner? Would I have been able to avoid the frustration and anxiety of my failed newspaper career? Honestly, I have no idea. But the right lesson in school, the right article online, the right video, might have sparked a fire and changed the course of my young life. Sometimes, a spark is all it takes.

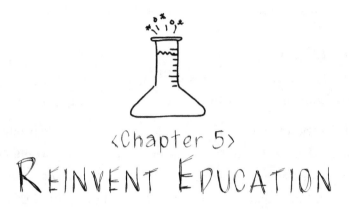

<Chapter 5>
REINVENT EDUCATION

Consider the atmosphere and expectations in today's typical classroom:

- Come to school on time.
- Get to class before the bell.
- Sit in your seat quietly.
- Don't talk while you work.
- Write the answers to all of the questions on your paper.
- Listen to the teacher and take notes.
- Leave when the bell rings, but you have to do more of the same work at home!

What were the two types of work that were declining in that MIT study? Routine and manual work. Right?

Let's think about what happens in that kind of work:

- Clock in.
- Go to your station.
- Don't talk.
- Do your work quietly.

- Forget creativity.
- Forget innovation.
- Clock out.
- Go home totally uninspired. (Okay, I may have taken some liberties with that last one, but you get the idea.)

Education today is driven by methods effective for producing good little factory workers, but the kind of work people do in today's workforce is *non-routine, interpersonal,* and *analytical.* Call me crazy, but something doesn't add up. The practices that persist in classrooms today certainly helped workers thrive during the Industrial Revolution, but the Industrial Revolution is over! The *digital* revolution is here. It's time our classrooms address the needs of the current and *future* marketplace. Ditching those textbooks—as well as textbook mindsets about education—will go a long way to improve education in general, and will help individual teachers implement more effective and up-to-date teaching methods in their classrooms.

It's easy to write and talk about reinventing education. In discussion, we can make the future whatever we want it to be. We can criticize the parts we find irrelevant and call for changes to the education system as a whole. But when the rubber meets the road, what does reinvention mean for us as educators? How can we make our classrooms and schools relevant?

I've already noted how unprecedented access to information and thought-leaders provides amazing opportunities for learning and discussion. No longer do teachers and schools have a corner on disseminating information. From independent study to massive, open, online courses (MOOCs) that provide college-level education (minus the high tuition fees), learning can take place anytime, anywhere. In schools, technology can enhance our lessons. Students can do a quick Google search on topics from class and can discover facts and concepts we, as teachers, have yet to learn. That's not to say we're not well-educated, thorough educators. It just shows the breadth and depth of the Internet. In fact, I believe one of our most important roles might not be answering questions, but helping students discover the right questions and showing them where and how to find the answers themselves. We must guide students to act on and use the information that's available to them. Additionally, we must teach our students the skill of adaptation. Alvin Toffler explained in *Future Shock*, "The illiterate of the twenty-first century will not be those who cannot read and write. The illiterate will be those who cannot learn, unlearn, and relearn." His message applies to teachers as well. If we can't unlearn and relearn, education is headed for irrelevance. Quickly.

Will Richardson wrote an excellent little book titled *Why School? How Education Must Change When Learning and Information Are Everywhere.* As I read it, my mind filled with ideas for changing the way I teach. Some of my methods, I realized, weren't relevant and needed updating.

I was learning, unlearning, and relearning.

In *Why School?*, Richardson includes comments from his interview with Larry Rosenstock, the founder of High Tech High, an innovative school in San Diego, California. Rosenstock suggests a paradigm shift for educators: Don't tell kids what to learn and don't tell them when and how to learn it. Doing so smothers their passion for learning and fails to develop the ability to guide their own learning.

After reading Richardson's book, one of my first, doubtful thoughts was: Self-directed learning fits wonderfully for some content areas, but it isn't so easy for others. Take my class, high school Spanish, for example. Learning a new language isn't unlike improving in sports, music, or any other skill. It takes lots of repetition. Learning Spanish can feel a lot like practicing free throws to improve your shot. In shooting all these "free throws," where is discovery? Where does the "learn what drives you" philosophy come into play? For me, this is where unlearning and relearning must come to the forefront. I had to get creative and find opportunities to allow students to take control of their language learning. I realized one way I can do this is through custom vocabulary lessons. Students help pick the words we learn based on what's interesting to them.

No matter what subject or grade you teach, you can think beyond the textbook. You can unlearn, relearn, and find ways to improve your students' learning experience.

Change Starts with You

Can individual teachers single-handedly change the way kids learn in schools around the world? Well, yes and no. We can't move the complacent teachers and administrators out of their comfort zones. We might not be able to quickly shift entire schools and districts on our own. But we can start the change... even if only in our own classrooms.

Large doors swing on very small hinges. If we can start the change with our own students, we can tout the benefits of our own personal education reform to others. We can take our stories and share results through social media, in personal conversations, or by blogging. What we *can't* do is keep our great work hidden within our classroom walls. If the education community and public perception are going to change, people have to see what forward-thinking teachers are doing. Otherwise, how will they know the magic that happens when kids get excited about learning?

How can we reinvent education? The easier question might be, "How can we *not* reinvent education?" The answer there is simple: Don't do anything. Let frustration keep you from taking action. And definitely don't speak up about what should change and how modern classrooms should operate.

The world continues to change. To keep up with it, our students desperately need us to ditch our textbook ways of looking at education. They need us to get in touch with current and future marketplace demands so they are equipped for real life. Reinventing education will take work, no question. But doing nothing and maintaining the status quo, puts our students at a loss.

ON THE BLOG:
10 THOUGHTS ON HOW TO GO DIGITAL AND WHY WE SHOULD

<Chapter 6>

WE ARE NO LONGER THE GATEKEEPERS

Decades ago, if you wanted to learn, school was the only place to go to access learning resources. Schools housed libraries full of books with seemingly endless amounts of information. They provided textbooks designed to help teachers deliver information to eager students.

Decades ago, teachers were the gatekeepers to learning. They held the keys to the library. They kept the textbooks and were revered for all the knowledge trapped in their brains. These experts presented streams of information to be copied down in spiral-bound notebooks. Teachers could be the "sage on the stage" because they were almost the only act in town.

Decades ago, a secure future required a college degree. Colleges had more experts, *professors*: teachers with sophisticated degrees who wore blazers with elbow patches. Students went to college, lived on campus within arm's reach of all of that information, and devoted themselves to full-time learning.

To recap: If you wanted an education, you went to school. If you wanted the American Dream, you went to college. If you went to college and earned a degree, your spot in the middle class was all but secured.

Oh, how things have changed.

Some teachers cling to their "gatekeeper of information" status with both fists and white knuckles. One such teacher was Dr. Roberts, a history professor whose class my wife and I took in college. (Roberts is not his real name.) This man taught for decades, during which time his teaching methods never varied. Nor did he update his notes. Each day, when he arrived in class, he set his briefcase on the desk and took out a stack of yellowed, handwritten pages. After arranging his desk, he sat in front of the class and delivered his notes for an hour. I tried frantically to follow his lecture and write my own notes but generally failed at both. When he finished, he tucked his papers into his briefcase and presumably returned them to their file-folder home, where they obviously enjoyed a nice long life.

When Dr. Roberts was hired to teach history (years before I arrived in his class), the "stand and deliver" technique was popular. Students came from far and wide to hear him lecture on world history. In his prime, Dr. Roberts *was* the gatekeeper to information. With the gatekeeper's permission, you could pass through the gate. For the record, I passed through Dr. Roberts' information gate with the worst grade of my collegiate career. If his like-minded colleagues are still teaching today, I hope they have replaced their yellowed pages and jumped on the information superhighway. I hope they have gone digital. (I have my doubts, though.) Why? Because teachers, even the ones with fancy elbow patches, are no longer the gatekeepers of information.

From Gatekeepers to Guides

Some of the best colleges have opened their virtual doors to outstanding, high-demand courses. Schools like Stanford, MIT, and Carnegie Mellon conduct free courses online. Most of these massive, open, online classes (MOOCs) allow students to enroll at any time and work at their own pace. Without paying tuition, students can receive a top-rate education and earn badges or certificates of completion. MOOCs generally don't offer official college credit, but that may be coming.

The education of our students' dreams—no, an education beyond their wildest dreams—awaits them online. It doesn't involve getting in to the right class with the good professor. It doesn't require sitting through a boring, irrelevant lecture. The gates have been flung wide and students can walk right into the land of information, peruse its various sections, take what they want, and come and go as they please.

My daughters, ages nine and seven, were recently wowed by a yo-yo presenter at their school. His show included some fancy tricks along with encouragement for the students to become champions at school and in life. Guess what really stuck in my girls' minds… the yo-yo tricks! They immediately wanted to learn how to do those tricks themselves. So, where do they go to learn? Cassie, my nine-year-old, came home that afternoon and asked, "Dad, can I go on YouTube to learn how to do a sleeper?" (A sleeper is when you make the yo-yo spin on the end of its string so you can do the cool tricks, like "walk the dog" and "around the world.") She's in third grade and has already used YouTube to learn how to crochet, knit, and do magic tricks. So why not yo-yo tricks? Notice, she didn't ask me how to throw a sleeper. I've been trying for years and still can't do it on a traditional yo-yo.

We watched some videos together, and even though we can't do it yet—throwing a sleeper is hard—we're getting closer. It will take practice, but at least we know the mechanics of the trick.

The YouTube phenomenon has affected classes around the world for years, but many teachers have not yet come to terms with it. YouTube—along with Wikipedia and Google searches—are many kids' first lines of attack when they want to learn something new. Examples:

- If they want to learn how to build a roof on their Minecraft buildings, they'll look for a YouTube video to show them.

- If they see a reference to a historical figure on their favorite TV show and want more information, they'll find it on Wikipedia.

- A quick trivia fact brought up in conversation with friends can be settled with a Google search on their smartphones.

Students don't go to the library or to their teachers to learn these things. They go to the Web, where people from every walk of life contribute content. The fact that the information isn't peer-reviewed or vetted by professionals doesn't bother kids. And I am going to suggest it shouldn't bother you (much) either. Most of the time, the community of users at YouTube, Wikipedia, and similar sites keep the content honest and accurate.

Before you get discouraged and start to think that all this free access to information is going to make you redundant, listen up: Your students need you. Yes, they can turn to the Internet to find facts, ideas, and opinions. But they need your assistance and guidance to discover the resources that will help them find their passions. In that respect, students don't need teachers to tell them what to learn. What they need are mentors and guides to help them discover what they want to learn and who they want to be. To an extent, our role in education has shifted from teacher to virtual-learning, travel guides.

ON THE BLOG:
10 Ways YouTube can
Engage Your Classes Now

<Chapter 7>
REAL-WORLD SKILLS

Educators face a daunting task. Not only must we learn, unlearn, and relearn our methods and continually evaluate and update our toolboxes, but we must also prepare students for the ever-changing career frontier. A report from U.S. Department of Labor predicts that sixty-five percent of today's schoolchildren eventually will be employed in jobs that have yet to be created.[1] That means we must teach students the skills they'll need to solve problems we've never before seen, and won't see for years.

Even today's technology skills may be obsolete before students graduate, let alone before they reach the workforce. When I was a journalism student in college, my professors tried to prepare me for the technological real world by teaching me how to create databases, use word processors, and save files to Iomega Zip disks, which ceased to exist soon after I graduated college.

Thankfully, some skills are timeless. They've been relevant for decades, even centuries. They will continue to be pertinent well into the future. Regardless of the changes that technology is sure to bring in the coming years, the following skills will serve our students well as they enter the real world.

1. Adding value. Analyze what's already out there. Figure out what's not. Then, contribute something original and worthwhile. A surefire way to get noticed—and avoid getting lost in the noise that competes for attention in the workplace—is to help people in new or unique ways.

In the classroom, we can praise novel contributions in conversations, student work, and projects.

2. Creating content online. The Internet is a medium unlike anything we've seen before. It allows anyone to become a public speaker, a movie director, an author, or an entrepreneur. A handful of skills can prepare students for a vast array of opportunities in business, in influencing others, and in life in general. For example, knowing how to upload a blog post and how to reach others through social media are basic skills for the next generation. If students don't know how to harness the power of the Internet, those doors can't be opened.

In the classroom, we can help students learn how to design websites, create videos, post blogs, and publish ebooks. More importantly, we can teach them the process of learning these things.

3. Continuously listening and watching for new ideas. You never know when a passing comment from someone or an innocuous sentence in an article may be the inspiration for a life-changing project or opportunity. Attentiveness is a skill that will always be in demand and will always create success for those who work at leveraging it.

In the classroom, we can make a game out of finding worthy ideas in unlikely places.

65 percent of today's schoolchildren eventually will be employed in jobs that have yet to be created.

4. Glamorizing hard work. Overnight successes aren't normal, but they receive more hype than the slow-and-steady approach. True success is often built from consistent, quality work over time. Hard work pays. Success stories don't happen because people get lucky. (Well, most of the time they don't.) As Thomas Edison said, "Opportunity is missed by most people because it is dressed in overalls and looks like work."

In the classroom, we can lavish praise on a student when he or she does exceptionally detailed, thought-provoking, or thorough work.

5. Turning wasted time to productive time. I'm a runner, and I noticed that my forty-five-minute to two-hour runs allowed me to think, but didn't yield as much productivity as parking myself in front of my computer. I started carrying a digital voice recorder with me. With it, I can dictate ideas as they come to me so I won't forget them. In fact, that's how I prepared for this chapter. I created productivity where it didn't exist.

In the classroom, we can help students find ways to make the most of their waking hours. Time spent on television, movies, video games, and the phone is fertile ground for finding a bit of extra productivity.

6. Cultivating relationships. We all can learn from others. But relationships can stagnate. Maintaining contact helps keep our connections with others active and it helps us grow. Business and life are still people-oriented, and they always will be.

In the classroom, we can create opportunities for collaboration—team activities, whole-class projects—especially those that reach beyond completing a worksheet together.

7. Being financially responsible. If an opportunity presents itself, we may be bound in chains if we're stuck in debt. If a cross-country move, an important tool, or a strategic plane ticket will help us get to the next level, we can't be debilitated by our bills. Anything we can do to show students the power of financial freedom will pay dividends.

In the classroom, we can make the connection between financial stability and students' goals.

8. Staying on the cutting edge. Follow trend-setters. Watch innovators. Know the new products. Read the news. Pay attention to what's going on so the world doesn't pass you by.

In the classroom, we can use new tools and discuss how new information is relevant to their work.

9. Maintaining the balance between professionalism and being a real person. The marketplace depends on goods and services, time management, and professional work. It's also made of real people who appreciate humor and want to connect on a personal level. It's important to know where the line is drawn, and connected, between the two.

In the classroom, we can have honest one-on-one conversations with students when they stray from that professional/personal line.

10. Becoming a twenty-four-hour worker. No, you don't have to work every waking moment. But today's world doesn't sleep. E-commerce, social media, and business in general has become an on-demand commodity. The best workers know how to make themselves available in short spurts, many times a day instead of working eight hours and shutting off.

In the classroom, we can give students opportunities to connect outside of class digitally or face-to-face.

A disconnect exists between what the workforce wants from graduates and what schools teach them to be and do. Math, science, social studies, and English are important, but employers are also looking for communication, digital literacy, problem-solving, and creative-thinking skills. By reaching for these real-world skills whenever possible, we'll be ditching our textbook concept of school and creating something far more relevant.

SECTION 2

DITCH THAT MINDSET

Schools haven't changed a lot in the last century. In that time, teachers have passed down ideas and observed practices from other teachers, creating an academic culture similar to what our parents and grandparents experienced.

Attitude and mindset are huge determining factors in our success and the success of our students. A few changes can mean the difference between a hostile, cold classroom atmosphere and a warm, welcoming one. If educators would open their minds to new approaches to how education is done, big changes in schools could drastically accelerate. Those educators could also streamline their lives and appreciate their careers more.

In the following section, we'll examine our mindsets toward what we do as educators, ditch those that don't serve us, and replace them with more productive ones.

‹Chapter 8›
MAKE IT PERSONAL

Who was the first person you looked for in your school's new yearbook?

If you're like most people, the answer is: *you.*

You probably checked the index to see what page you were on. You looked at the class picture section to see your mugshot and make sure your name was spelled correctly. You searched for your face in candid photos to see how you looked playing sports, participating in class, or hanging out with your friends.

Who did you look for next? Your friends and siblings.

Even as adults, we want to see ourselves in everything in which we're engaged. We're concerned about our image and about how we look and sound to people… even if we don't admit it.

Do you think our students are any different? I teach high school students, and if that's not a major egocentric time of life, then my hairline isn't disappearing like a setting sun.

If our students want to find themselves when they open a yearbook, wouldn't they want to find themselves in our instruction as well?

Blaine Ray, the creator of a conversational method of teaching world languages, explains that students listen if we're talking about them. "They will pay attention better, and they will remember what you have taught better," he writes in *Fluency Through TPR Storytelling*. "Bring in events from their lives. Have mini-stories contain important school events or national events. Talk about food the students eat. This is all part of 'personalization.'"

As a world languages teacher, I can talk about practically anything in my classes as long as I use vocabulary and grammar concepts we've covered or that they can figure out on their own. So, from time to time, I'll make up stories in class with my students as the stars. We'll talk about things that are important to them, like the day when fog surprisingly delayed school for two hours.

I don't like using worksheets and activities out of textbooks. (Surprise, surprise, right?) When I need a practice activity, I prefer to write my own content, and my students are often the main characters. Their lives are the plotline. If I have multiple class periods of the same subject, it takes only a "find and replace" in my word processor to change the names.

Personalizing activities in a class is pretty easy in world languages, but the principle also applies to other areas of study.

- Social studies teachers can equate the conflict and social ramifications of historic events to students' lives.
- Science teachers can personalize processes and concepts by having students act them out or by comparing them to their own lives ("mitochondria are kind of like the Red Bull that Jack drinks to stay awake late at night playing Xbox").
- Literature has so many parallels to our students' social lives that it's pretty easy to personalize what they're reading in class.

Connecting with Questions

Sometimes, getting personal with students simply requires asking questions that grab their attention. You know, the kind of questions that have been asked for ages but have no clear answer. Questions like:

Why do we hurt the ones we love?

Why is Pepsi better than Coke (or vice versa)?

How do you manage eye contact with a stranger as you walk down an empty hall with them?

What's my purpose?

Why am I here?

Where am I headed?

Everyone has an opinion about those kinds of questions. We all can connect with them regardless of our backgrounds. But instead of asking them in our classes, we ask the "right" questions.

The questions that allow us to hit our content standards.

The questions that prepare our students for tests.

The questions that help us unpack the content we want to teach.

Maybe we need to focus less on asking the right questions and start asking the relevant questions.

Sure, when you're teaching about Julius Caesar, you need to ascertain who betrayed and killed him. But let's connect the concept to our students' lives. You could ask:

- Why does a boy ask a girl to the prom and then discard her for another date a week before the big dance?
- When have you been betrayed in your own life?
- What are the alternatives to betrayal, and why would, or why wouldn't, someone take a less relationship-damaging approach?

> Maybe we need to focus less on asking the right questions and start asking the relevant questions.

Those kinds of questions help students really see themselves in the subject matter. They connect kids to the content, regardless of their backgrounds, which is very often the reason for teaching a topic in the first place! Just imagine the kinds of responses you could get with questions that made the material relevant.

In basic algebra, students do operations to both sides of an equation to solve the problem. That's balance. If the balance isn't maintained correctly, you can't solve the problem accurately. Where else in life is balance necessary? Make the connection. Has anyone paid so much attention to a boyfriend or girlfriend that their family or friend relationships suffered? A five-minute side conversation about balance in life helps students view the material from a different angle. Plus, more importantly, those kinds of questions get them thinking about character. Asking them incorporates the big-picture thinking our students struggle with and probably need the most guidance on navigating.

Will a conversation about balance in life help algebra students understand how to solve problems? Some educators may scoff and say the approach sounds like fluff. But if you're an algebra teacher who's brave enough to test the theory, I bet you'll be surprised at the connection your students will make between balance in life and in solving math problems.

Social studies teacher Kari Catanzaro made personal connections to her junior high unit on landforms by creating a musical playlist of songs with landforms in them. She included "Ain't

No Mountain High Enough," "The Climb," "Proud Mary," and "Mountain Music." The playlist sparked a discussion about the figurative use of those landforms in music and life: an angry person who erupted like a volcano, the ups and downs of life which are like hills, or the place in our lives—like our own bedroom—that are like an oasis.

"The kids really got into it," she said. "Even though I didn't tell them to, some shared what landform their life represented with each other, and I saw compassion and empathy and connections. It gave us a real life lesson using landforms vocabulary. I will definitely do it again!"

If we can ditch our textbooks, at least momentarily, and connect to our students' lives through our content, we can help them answer those big questions: What is my purpose? Why am I here? Where am I headed?

Then, they'll see themselves in what they're learning. They'll make the real-life connections. And they'll internalize the content and understand how it matters to their lives. Isn't that what we're really working toward?

<Chapter 9>
Fun and Magic

"Where Dreams Come True" is the perfect slogan for Disney Parks. Fun and magic fill the air and pixie dust permeates everything at Disney World. Its atmosphere points right back to the founder, Walt Disney. He was an innovator. He wanted his guests to feel as if they were in a whole different world when they stepped inside the gates. He wanted them to experience something magical.

Recently, when I took my family to Disney World, I learned lessons I can incorporate into my classes to create a fun, magical experience: set the scene, don't forget the details, and place a priority on customer service.

Set the scene. When you walk into a Disney attraction, you can see Walt Disney's views on stepping into a different world. The scene for the "Twilight Zone Tower of Terror" ride at Disney Hollywood Studios is a posh hotel that's been abandoned. The swanky furniture and suitcases covered in dust and cobwebs create a believable atmosphere and make you feel as if you're part of a real experience.

Don't forget the little details. The paved walkways at Disney World caught my attention. How many theme parks across the world leave pathways bland rather than using them to add the experience? Not Disney. In Animal Kingdom, for example, you'll find animal footprints and leaf impressions in the pavement.

Customer service is top priority. The vast majority of Disney staff (aka *cast members*) go all out to be helpful and cordial. Why? Because it's the happiest place on earth! (Okay, technically that title belongs to Disneyland, but it applies here, too!) The cast members are obviously happy, and they know how important it was that *you* are happy.

I see *fun* as an intermediate goal. It's not the end goal; if it were, my title would be comedian. And I would probably not stay in that line of work very long! But part of my role is helping kids enjoy themselves. If I do a good job, they seem to pay attention better and work harder when it's time to get serious.

Here are a few ways I incorporate fun into my class:

- We answer questions on small whiteboards from time to time. To test their markers, I'll give students a minute to draw a picture of whatever they'd like and I'll reward them with a sticker. (Yes, stickers are still an effective motivational tool for teenagers!)

- In my class, we write blogs and comment on one another's posts. To make sure everyone gets comments, students pass cards with their names on them around the room. Before passing a card, they'll hold it in their right hand. Then with their left hand they'll cover one eye and make a pirate sound. Then they'll tuck the card in their sleeves like they're doing a magic trick—just for fun. Then they'll pass the card to the next person.

- I love to teach Spanish with storytelling. We can make up any kind of story imaginable as long as we're using the vocabulary and grammar we're studying that week. One way to be sure they're listening, is to make my students the stars of the stories and have them do crazy, fun, unbelievable things. Another way to keep their attention is with props. A favorite class memory of two former students—a couple of tough farm boys—is when I wrestled a stuffed fish on the floor, and made it look like the fish was winning!

Teach Like a PIRATE author Dave Burgess offers two key points of advice that have inspired me to bring fun and magic into the classroom. He asks, "If your students didn't have to be there, would you be teaching in an empty room?" Dave says he has had a handful of days in his class, including the Lunar Landing and Sixties Party days, for which he could have sold tickets. Imagine the powerful learning that can happen when students are *that* engaged.

He also notes that we aren't simply in the business of delivering information. His advice: "Don't just teach a lesson, create an experience." The varied and epic lessons Dave taught in his social studies classroom included simulating a speakeasy, pulling a red, lacy bra out of a Victoria's Secret bag, and cramming dozens of students into a cardboard box. These tactics weren't just about shock factor; each taught a specific, important part of his curriculum.

Most kids are naturally curious and want to have a good time… even if that means that they learn something, too. In the summer of 2014, just after presenting a conference session on making global connections by using video chats in the classroom, a teacher in Canada contacted me. She was dying to do a Mystery

Skype activity that day. (A Mystery Skype is an activity during which two classes try to guess where in the world the other is geographically located.)

I said yes, even though I didn't have any participants yet. I had just left my classroom of teachers and didn't know where I was going to sit down to do this Mystery Skype, let alone who was going to help me.

So where did I go first? The cafeteria. The student helpers for the conference were hanging out there and were up for some fun. Even though they weren't officially in school, these kids had a great time, and they tapped into their problem-solving and geography skills.

If I did an optional Mystery Skype at a school, would I be teaching to an empty room? Not a chance! It's way too fun!

Fun and magic are powerful tools to wield. Unfortunately, they've almost been dirty words throughout the history of education. We are competing with the lure of constant marketing and on-demand entertainment for students' attention. Let's ditch those old textbook ideas of stodginess and formality. We *can* energize what we do at school.

ON THE BLOG:
GET THE FREE EBOOK: *THE DIGITAL PIRATE* TO LEARN MORE ABOUT TECH AND PIRATE TEACHING.

‹Chapter 10›
Build Respect and Relationships

I received a lot of advice as a new teacher. Advice such as, "Don't smile until Thanksgiving," and "Don't let students see the 'real you' too much." You know, those textbook suggestions some veteran teachers feel compelled to pass on to newbies.

There's one bit of advice that I accepted early in my career, but have slowly changed my stance on over time. (Not "Don't smile until Thanksgiving." I break that one the first day of school every year.) The warning I eventually decided to reject is, "Don't be your students' friend."

The well-intentioned, time-honored belief is, students need us to be their teachers, not their friends; they already have lots of friends. And I get that. In fact, I abode by this rule because the reasoning made sense to me. But a couple of experiences changed my perspective.

First, a presenter at a conference I attended made a statement that raised some serious questions in my mind. (I wish I remember who it was because I'd love to give him/her credit.) The statement was: "Kids don't learn from people they don't like." *No way*, I thought at the time. *Students learn from good teachers because they are masters of their content, have sound pedagogy, and deliver quality instruction. Right?*

Second, at a swimming coaches' conference, a speaker asked us if we thought it was important for our athletes to like us. He divided the room, and we moved to one side or the other, depending on whether or not we believed students needed to like their coaches. I moved to the "Your athletes don't have to like you" side. *Good coaches aren't always liked if they do the right thing*, I thought. To my surprise, the majority of the most successful coaches moved to the *other* side of the room. These *friendship fans* included coaches of state champions and one local coach who had won several consecutive sectional championships. My brain went into overdrive at the realization that I needed to rethink my philosophies and, perhaps, change my approach.

After several more years of teaching, here's the conclusion I've reached: a lot of being a good teacher is being a good friend. Just as with our personal relationships, teaching involves respecting others, treating each other right, and having each other's best interest in mind.

Your Students Need Good Friends

You see, we all have an account at the Relationship Bank and Trust. We have accounts with everyone who is important to us: family members, friends, students, and co-workers. How can you make a deposit? Empathize, be there through tough times, and lift up others. Withdrawals consist of hurtful comments and acts of selfishness. And let me tell you from experience—the withdrawals are always *much* bigger than the deposits. It takes an abundance of deposits to get that relationship account back to where it was.

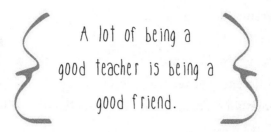

A lot of being a good teacher is being a good friend.

This Relationship Bank and Trust idea makes me think of a former student. Let's call him Jeremy. He played football and wrestled. He was, and still is, just about the easiest guy to get along with you'll ever meet. He treats everyone like a real person. Jeremy wasn't overly interested in Spanish, but because of his great attitude, we had a mutual respect and admiration for each other.

Jeremy claimed a hat from my classroom. And it was his hat. He knew it. I knew it. This hat wasn't expensive or even impressive. It was a plastic cowboy hat I got at Texas Roadhouse on my birthday one year. Jeremy grabbed it out of my room one day and wore it in the student cheer block during the homecoming basketball game. Pretty regularly, he wore it in my room during class, which was just fine by me. He wasn't hurting anything, and it helped us connect. When Jeremy graduated, you can guess what I gave him as a graduation gift… yep, the plastic Texas Roadhouse cowboy hat. He appreciated that hat more than any greeting card I could have picked out, because it showed him I really did care about him as an individual. The gift was one more deposit in our mutual account. (Of course, if the card had $100 in it, he'd have been all over it.)

As teachers, it's easy to let our focus drift from the students who really need us to the ones who raise their hands most, score highest on our tests, and really get our content. Those hard-driving students thrive whether our teaching skills are mediocre or fantastic. Jeremy didn't graduate at the top of his class. He was sharp, but he didn't "play the game of school" well enough to earn a stellar report card. For him, a little extra attention and *friendship* meant the difference between simply surviving school and actually learning something. For me, the time and effort of being a friend is an excellent investment.

An exchange between Joe Redish, a physics professor at the University of Maryland, and Lewis Elton, a famous physicist, illustrates the need to connect with all students, particularly those who struggle. As a friend and caring mentor, Elton asked Redish how his teaching was going. Redish replied that it was going well, but he felt most effective with students "who do really well and are motivated" about physics. To which Elton responded, "They're the ones who don't really need you."

Why show students you care? Because, they need you. And they need good friends.

- A good friend brings a smile on a rough day.

- A good friend follows up on important issues. ("Hey, how did that go?" "Have you gotten around to that? I know it was important to you.")

- A good friend cares about his/her friend's life and well-being.

- A good friend matters to his/her friends.

I know that many of my high school students don't have a lot of good friends. Sometimes I can help fill that role. Other times, I have to be their teacher first and do what's best for them and the integrity of their grades or the school. As a teacher, I must maintain my objectivity. I have to treat and grade each student fairly, and I can't show bias. We're not meant to hang out with students at the mall or attend kids-only parties at their homes. In the student-teacher relationship, the teacher needs to maintain role of responsible adult looking out for the best interest of the student. Teachers can assume some characteristics of a good friend for students, but behaving like a child in order to be a child's friend is going too far.

It's up to me to care about my students. That's my choice. I've had many school years start off great—and finish with a bang! A huge part of the success in those years was due to the conscious effort I made loving my students, smiling, and showing them they matter to me. And, more importantly, being a good friend.

On the Blog:
4 Hospitality Principles that can Transform Our Classrooms

<Chapter 11>
Win and Influence Students

Why did you become a teacher?

Was it for the hours? The fame? The paycheck?

Probably not.

Was the reason, instead, a heartfelt desire to make a difference in the lives of children?

If so, that's influence. We don't just want to teach content. We want to influence lives.

One of the epic tomes on the subject, *How to Win Friends and Influence People* by Dale Carnegie, shaped my personal and teaching life in a substantial way. Its words, though penned in 1936, still hold the same weight of truth today. I took the Dale Carnegie Course in high school and am still using the human relations and public speaking skills I learned from it. For instance, one skill I learned was how to prepare, practice, and deliver talks. (My father, the facilitator for my Dale Carnegie Course, called the presentations "talks," because the term "speeches" struck fear in students' hearts.) I've since served as a graduate assistant for the course multiple times, and each session I'm reminded of how Carnegie's principles relate to education. So many of them feel like common sense! It's a shame the book isn't required reading for pre-service teachers. Carnegie would do more to positively shape teachers than many of the requisite curriculum and law texts.

If you haven't read *How to Win Friends and Influence People*, I highly recommend you do so. In the meantime, consider how the following six lessons Carnegie teaches could help you in your goal to make a difference in your students' lives.

1. Make the other person feel important—and do it sincerely.
Offer more than a quick "good job." Your students can see right through obligatory praise. But sincere, honest comments make students feel important and are powerful deposits in your account at Relationship Bank and Trust. Each "this is great work because…" or "I liked your effort in that match last night because…" or "you'll do great because…" adds to your balance. The more you deposit into that account, the stronger your relationships will become. For many students, the pointed praise and attention they receive from you may be the only encouragement they get all day—maybe all week.

2. If you are wrong, admit it quickly and emphatically.
Admitting being wrong scares teachers, and people in general, to death. I know of some teachers who will explain away their errors to protect their position as the boss or ruler of the class. That may have worked in the past, but today, a quick Google search can

We don't just want to teach content. We want to influence lives.

prove a teacher wrong in seconds. Showing that we're real, fallible humans goes a long way toward building trust. And as Carnegie explains, a quick, emphatic "I was wrong" takes the fight out of a conflict and often disarms the most hostile objector.

I love to give students the opportunity to teach me new words in Spanish. When I don't know a word and they can look it up and teach it to me, pride swells inside them, even if you can't see it on the outside. Letting a student show you where you made a mistake, and where he or she was right, counts for double pride points.

3. Get the other person saying "yes, yes" immediately. This is subtle, yet powerful. Getting people to engage in the simple act of saying "yes" puts them in a more positive mindset. Carnegie's book documents sales calls where the salesman starts his pitch with simple questions—factual ones or those with obvious "yes" answers. All the "yes" answers build momentum, putting the potential client in a more positive mood. The "yes, yes" tool should be in every teacher's tool belt—and within easy reach. The approach may not work every time, but it can be very effective in shifting your students into a receptive mindset.

4. Talk about your own mistakes before criticizing others. We were once students, too. We had that youthful, effervescent, hard-to-contain enthusiasm as second graders. We were unsure, awkward, hormonal teenagers at some point, too. I made my fair share of mistakes going through school. Reminding students they're not the only ones who err goes a long way. Carnegie wrote, "It isn't nearly so difficult to listen to a recital of your faults if the person criticizing begins by humbly admitting that he, too, is far from impeccable."

5. Ask questions instead of giving direct orders. Everyone likes to feel like they have a say in the decision-making process.

At most schools, kids generally don't wield much control. *Asking* them to do something instead of *telling* them to do it is a small gesture, but it can save and build relationships over time. Simply adding a "would you" or "do you mind" to requests humanizes the teacher-student interaction. Sometimes, the subtlety of the "ask, not demand" approach is lost on a student. When I get a "no" answer or am ignored, it usually takes only a quick explanation (with a smile) that I can either ask nicely or demand, to get the student's compliance.

6. Dramatize your ideas. Act in bold and visual ways, and your class and lessons will stand out in students' memories. *In How to Win Friends and Influence People,* Carnegie told the story of a cash register salesman who suggested that a grocer was losing money with each transaction using old-fashioned registers. The salesman actually threw pennies on the floor, showing the grocer how much money he was losing with each customer. "Merely stating the truth isn't enough," Carnegie wrote. "The truth has to be made vivid, interesting, dramatic. You have to use showmanship. The movies do it. Television does it. And you will have to do it if you want attention."

Whether or not they acknowledge it, as teachers we have enormous influence over our students. By leveraging these ideas to help students make smart decisions, we can guide them to become the best possible versions of themselves and create a positive classroom culture.

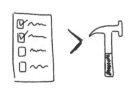

<Chapter 12>

Choose Task Over Tool

Technology is flashy. It's trendy.

iPads, Chromebooks, and smartphones make us look good just by using them in class. Tech tools put us on the cutting edge of innovation. Or, at least that's how they make us feel.

The cutting edge is where so many people want to be, but is flashy technology *really* the way to get there?

Yes, technology can be a catalyst to great things. It can make us and our students more efficient. For example, by using the computers in my classroom:

- My students can collaborate quickly and efficiently in written form.
- I can do lightning-quick, formative assessments to gauge student progress.
- I can grade and enter grades for those assessments faster than I could by hand.

Look at how technology has changed in the past few decades. When I was a child, we learned about technology and our studies through educational games like Math Blaster and Oregon Trail.

> The mindset that fuels digital learning is: Good teaching trumps good tools.

Now, augmented reality and Twitter are part of daily life in the classroom. In both cases, one common thread emerges: Good teachers have used technology to accomplish their teaching goals.

But technology also has its limitations. Computers and tablets are not the be-all and end-all of great teaching and learning in the classroom. Take bell-ringer activities, for example. A quick question on Socrative.com (an excellent, easy-to-use, digital assessment tool) can provide a helpful evaluation of student retention. But when I had nine-year-old desktop computers in my classroom that took five minutes or more to boot up, what should have been a "quick" exercise consumed half the class period. Similarly, an "exit slip" on Socrative asks students to summarize and reflect on their learning at the end of the period. It works wonders for helping to cement a lesson in their brains and for letting me see what they actually learned. I can download their responses into a spreadsheet and quickly analyze the data. But Socrative isn't as fast as a show of hands; a hands-up poll (no technology needed) gets results in seconds. Plus, the hands all over the classroom display easy-to-grasp results.

The bottom line is that pedagogy must drive technology. The mindset that fuels digital learning is: Good teaching trumps good tools.

That maxim sometimes seems counter-intuitive to us techies. Technology gets the headlines. It gets the students' attention. It gets the superintendent's attention. It gets the community's attention. Twitter posts by educators teem with tech tools to try in class: the apps, the websites, and the devices. It's easy to lose our focus. But we must focus on our students and what's best for them in the long run.

In my years as a high school teacher, I have come to appreciate and respect the sanctity of the class period—one hundred eighty days, forty-five minutes at a time. Finite and fleeting—especially when those minutes are lost to interruptions, school assemblies, and field trips—class time is precious. I can't afford to waste time on fancy tools that don't advance my students' education. If I'm going to use any form of technology, it must improve my students' learning experience... quickly and effectively. Solid teaching trumps all. This is the cardinal rule we always come back to, for good reason.

So, fellow educator, we must stay judicious. We can't give in to the glitter, the flash, or the shine of tech tools that don't make our students better people. I, at times, have felt shame for using traditional techniques and foregoing a sophisticated gadget, website, or app. But then I remember the technology is a tool, not the goal. The learning experiences are the focus.

Don't be ashamed. Efficiency and effectiveness are key. Our students are key. Don't be afraid to integrate technology and innovative teaching ideas, but don't get lost in the glitter of the next big thing in educational technology.

The real "next big thing" is sitting in your classroom ready to learn. It's the next generation. Don't forsake it for the flash.

ON THE BLOG:
6 REASONS YOU SHOULD DITCH YOUR EDTECH

<Chapter 13>

WHAT EVERY TECH-USING EDUCATOR MUST KNOW

Adding technology to education comes at a cost. It takes a lot of money, time, and effort. Still, so many schools insist on using technology, even if they don't have a clear vision for how they want to implement it.

Done well, technology integration can transform classes and enhance learning. The right kinds of tech give students experiences they never could have otherwise.

But when it's done poorly, students are handed what Canadian principal and education speaker George Couros calls a "$1,000 pencil"—a costly piece of equipment they use to do the same things they were doing with pencils and paper.

So how can you get the most bang for your technology buck? How can you make the most of the devices in our classrooms? A framework like the SAMR Model[1] can help you select, use, and evaluate the best technology for your classroom. (See Figure 1.) When you're considering whether to include a device or digital application to your lesson, put the tech to the test. What value will

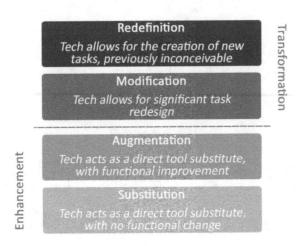

FIGURE 1: SAMR MODEL

it bring to your classroom? Will it be a substitution, augmentation, modification, or redefinition of what you're doing now?

Substitution means using technology as a direct tool substitute. Example: Typing papers on a typewriter instead of writing them by hand.

Augmentation occurs when technology is a direct tool substitute with functional improvement. Example: Typing those same papers with a word processor and using spell check.

Modification applies when technology allows for significant task redesign and changes everything. Example: Instead of typing papers, students could write a series of blog posts and allow fellow classmates to comment and engage in conversation.

Redefinition is what happens when technology allows for the creation of new, previously inconceivable tasks. Example: Sharing those blog posts with a global audience and engaging in comment dialogue with people all over the world.

SAMR's creator, Dr. Ruben Puentedura, founder of the education consulting firm Hippasus, puts substitution and augmentation in the "enhancement" group, and puts modification and redefinition in the "transformation" group. There's a reason for that.

I've found that the big struggle is the leap from augmentation to modification. The dashed line dividing the SAMR graphic is like a tall fence to climb... a fence with barbed wire at the top! (Okay, barbed wire may be a bit of an exaggeration, but sometimes it feels like an impossible hurdle!) Jumping that fence takes teachers out of the comfort of substitution and augmentation. In essence, they often end up throwing their previous activities out the window and creating new ones.

That's what modification asks of us: "significant task redesign." Design it again. Significantly. No teacher has time to put in all the effort of redesigning a task just to do the same thing as before in a different way. Instead, the goal is to do something greater, something that wasn't possible using traditional methods. And if the task was inconceivable without technology, you've just made the soaring leap to the redefinition level.

So, how do you make the leap over the tall fence? Here are several steps you can take:

1. Get crystal clear about your goals. What do you want your students to learn? What do you want them to be able to do? Try not to think of the *tasks* you want them to do; focus on the end *goal.*

2. Review your previous activities (if you had them) and identify what you liked about them. What made the most difference for students? What really got them thinking? Don't think in terms of "this worksheet was good" or "this chapter covered the subject well." Instead, focus on the students' *experiences* and the *gains made* because of a particular activity.

3. Match your goals and your favorite parts of previous activities to tools with similar strengths. Scan through lists of apps and websites with a discerning eye. They're all over the place. A few quick Internet searches will uncover several! Which tool(s) match or could support your essential goals or needs, even if you don't yet know how you're going to use it?

4. Keep an open mind. There are no bad questions during brainstorming. Similarly, any idea or digital tool that has the potential to help your students reach their goals is worth consideration. Exploring tech options is a process. *Embrace it*—even if you feel a bit uncertain. Consider it an adventure.

5. Generate several ideas for potential activities. List all the ways your students could use the technology to reach their goals. Then, narrow down the list by identifying the activities and ideas you like, and cross out those that aren't as appealing to you. Eventually, you'll find a few favorite ways for incorporating an app or device in your classroom.

6. Gather opinions. Provide your students with goals, some ideas for activities, and the tools to reach them. Then see what they think. They may give you new ideas, come up with different ways to follow through on your previous ideas, or suggest additional tools. Ask colleagues for input, or post your thoughts on social media to gather feedback.

7. Finalize your ideas and put them into action! Action is important, even if you don't feel like an expert on new tools yet. Students are pretty sharp and can help you work through the technical parts of your new plan. Remember, if they *do* help, that doesn't mean you're less of a teacher; it means you are learning *with* them! Jump in with both feet. Even if your first (or twenty-first) attempt doesn't work out perfectly—or blows up in your face—your students will appreciate your willingness to try new things.

8. Be flexible and be ready to change. If something flops early on, be ready to revise it or try it again the next day. We don't have to be perfect. The acronym FAIL (First Attempt In Learning) applies to teachers, too!

Reflect afterward on your new activities. Ask students what they liked about the activity and how well it helped them learn the subject or lesson.

Note: If you're thinking, *Wow, all of those steps sound like a lot of work!* don't worry. The steps above aren't a formal process that must be followed every time you want to introduce a tech tool in your classroom. Eventually, you will be able to quickly evaluate new ideas and tech uses in your mind. Taking the time, at least initially, to use this process will help you make the most of technology in your classroom. With all that money, time, and effort required, you want to earn maximum dividends on your investment.

10 Ways to Reach SAMR's Redefinition Level

1. **Cultural exchanges:** My students were fortunate to participate in a cultural exchange with a class in Spain. Students met in pairs via Skype to discuss predetermined topics and to just talk about whatever they wanted. They then wrote in their second language (Spanish or English) about the conversation and let the other students help correct their mistakes. I've written several posts about this exchange.[2]

2. **Public blogs:** Writing has always been at the core of many subjects. Blogs give students' writing a new, exciting potential audience: the world. Students can write in publicly accessible blogs and share them via any channels possible (e.g., school website, school newsletter, Twitter, Google Plus communities, listservs, etc.). Blog comments allow students to discuss ideas with people they would never otherwise meet.

3. **Global perspectives:** Students can connect with a class in another part of the world to discuss a historical event, preferably one that affects both of their countries. They can write facts about the event in a shared Google document, blog, or any other publishing tool and then share their opinions. They can compare how an event is perceived in different parts of the world and broaden their own perspective on world events.

4. **"Aid the community" competition:** In this competition, students from various countries engage in a project to tackle an issue in their communities (e.g. reducing their community's carbon footprint). Students share ideas on a website or a shared Google document, discuss ideas together via video chat on Skype, FaceTime, or Google Hangout, and partner with researchers at local universities or companies. They share

the findings of their yearlong endeavor in a documentary on YouTube.[3]

5. **Publishing ebooks:** Creating an ebook opens up students' work to a global audience in a way that was previously impossible. With digital production and distribution, students can share their hard work, research, and results with the world. iBooks Author[4], or any publishing platform that produces epub or PDF files (Microsoft Publisher, Google Apps, etc.), allows students to become published authors. Their ebooks can then be offered for free, or at a price to benefit a charity or other cause, through Amazon and other ebook sellers. (Inspired by Jon Smith's class.[5])

6. **Twitter writing:** Twitter, by nature, connects students to people from all walks of life and teaches brevity in writing with its 140-character limit. Students can engage in a collaborative writing project with students—or anyone, anywhere—via Twitter. Teachers can post a story starter with a hashtag, and participants can suggest ideas for the story's continuation. The result is a crowd-sourced story with a ready audience.[6]

7. **Sketchnoting:** If you've seen an RSA Animate video,[7] where an artist sketches visual notes based on a motivating speech, you've seen sketchnoting. Plenty of digital tools are available to sketchnote,[8] and sketchnotes can be shared with an audience for dialogue and idea creation.[9]

8. **Bookmark annotating:** Sites like Diigo.com allow users to bookmark sites and annotate over them. Previously, we had to rely on sticky notes and writing in margins for annotations, but now, students, or the teacher, can bookmark sites, write notes, and highlight important ideas right on the page. Tools like Diigo encourage discussion by allowing students and teachers to access one another's notes from anywhere.

9. **Nearpod presentation:** Nearpod.com totally revamps presentations. This app gives the presenter controls they don't have with a standard PowerPoint presentation (and it's free). Teachers send out the digital presentation to students' devices and control what they see. Students can interact and respond to the presentation, and the teacher can monitor student progress.

10. **The paperless classroom with Google Docs:** Instead of creating documents on paper, distributing them to students, and collecting them as assignments, students and teachers can function paperlessly. Documents in Google Apps, or Evernote, or other options, can be digitally organized and edited. They can be simultaneously shared and edited by any user. Users can even use chat windows and comment boxes to discuss content. They can all be accessed from anywhere, making teaching and learning a better, virtual experience.

‹Chapter 14›
GIVE STUDENTS CONTROL

My wife and I bought a house three doors down from our first home, and I have to admit, it was a dump. The previous owners left the place in shambles. It sat vacant after a foreclosure and neglect took its toll. The kitchen's peel-and-stick floor tiles curled and buckled around the 1950s-era metal cabinets. Yellow residue from cigarette smoke covered the walls. The upstairs carpets… well, to avoid completely grossing you out, let's just say they made the home practically uninhabitable.

After a winter spent tearing out, peeling, painting, and refinishing, we had vastly improved the house's appearance. It was finally a place where the word *home* aptly applied. And that's exactly what it became for the family of five who rented it. After pouring blood, sweat, and drywall mud into that house, it felt counterintuitive to hand over the keys to people we barely knew.

Thankfully, we had all-star renters. They didn't smoke. They didn't party. They didn't have pets. They paid their rent and told us they loved living in our house. They were, in fact, a landlord's dream.

But there was this funny thing about them. They didn't do anything to renovate our house. No new paint. No new carpet. No windows or doors or bathroom fixtures. They just lived in the house and paid the rent.

Funny? Okay, not really. They were tenants. Renters don't typically invest their time, money, or energy in the landlord's house. Working on the house doesn't improve their financial situation, so why bother? When tenants move out, they don't reap the rewards of a higher resale value because they didn't own the house.

My renters were exactly like my students.

Students don't want to take control of their education until they own it. Students either rent or own. The renters come to our classes because they have to be there. They don't see the connection between what we're selling—our content—and their own lives. They earn decent grades because their parents say they must. Or they don't bother earning good grades at all. Renter students pay only what's due… until something better comes along.

The owner students, though, act as dedicated caretakers of their educations. They take notes with the same meticulousness I used to install new trim on the freshly painted walls of my house. Their thoughtful questions add color, interest, and value to their educational experiences. They own their educations. They want to add value to their learning because they realize that's where they will live… and how they will one day earn a nice profit.

How do we get the renters to sign the deed and own their educations?

That's the million-dollar question.

The answer lies in helping them change their mindsets about school and study. For me, that means helping students see the relationship between what they're learning and where they want to be one day. Our goal should be to help students see the value of their studies in relation to their personal goals. As a foreign language teacher, I see lots of those relationships. College. Travel. Job marketability. Connecting to a world of people they couldn't otherwise. No matter what you teach, I'm sure you are well aware of all the ways your subject matter could help your kids succeed in life outside the classroom. We just have to get our students to see those connections.

Aside from making education relevant, one of the best ways to get kids to own their education is to hand it over to them. They know what they want to learn. They know what interests them. Why not turn students loose to learn on their own? Students like having a voice in what they do, and if they can see themselves in a project or activity, they're more likely to take ownership of it.

That said, the transition to student-led learning isn't smooth or easy; minor, or maybe major, catastrophes will likely ensue. Students' attention will stray. They will abuse time and resources. Count on it. They're kids and they're learning how this world works. That doesn't mean that we shouldn't turn over control. I'm convinced that the only reason we don't hand over control is because it's easier to hang on to the comfort of the status quo. But that approach will never yield the benefits we want for our students.

Despite the inevitable challenges, I encourage you to have faith that your students will do the right thing. Don't abandon your best ideas because some kid might make a bad decision. Let them choose what they will learn in your class. Give them the freedom to pursue an idea in their own ways. The results might surprise you.

Some teachers are awesome at letting students sit in the driver's seat of their own educations. One such teacher is Joy Kirr. She is a seventh-grade English/language arts teacher from Elk Grove,

Illinois. Kirr turns complete control of her classes over to her students one day a week during Genius Hour. Genius Hour is a spin-off of Google's famous Twenty-Percent Time program, in which Google employees are given twenty percent of their workday or workweek to pursue projects in their interests… provided those interests relate to Google's mission, of course. During Genius Hour, Kirr's students pick a topic about which they're enthusiastic. Then they research and pursue it.

In a more radical version of students pursuing their own interest, Don Wettrick, a teacher in Noblesville, Indiana, has created a class called "Innovation." Think of Joy Kirr's Genius Hour but for the entire class every day. Wettrick's students develop apps, make websites and create a digital presence online through social media. But Wettrick starts the process by teaching them how not to think like the average student. "Right now, it is natural for kids to be compliant, to sit and listen to what their teachers have to say without questioning," Wettrick said in an article about his class. "The system beats the creativity out of them. Kids have been trained that way. My first job is to unteach them."[1]

Another way of giving students control in the classroom is by not teaching. Katie Regan says she doesn't teach her tenth-grade enriched English class, and she's right. She is a conversation moderator. She is a technology travel guide. She is a personal trainer, motivating students to do the work themselves. A "sage on the stage" she is not. Some features of Regan's teaching include:

- Online teacher/student and student/student collaboration about thesis statements, outlines and more, through commenting.

- Flipped video lessons for new content. Students ask her for information available in those videos sometimes. "I keep telling them, 'I don't know! Watch the video again, or look it up!'" she says.

- Plenty of varied tech resources. Regan has access to iPad carts (a school iPad for every student) and a computer lab of PCs. She relies on Edmodo.com and Google Docs every day.

When students can see how their education relates to the big picture of life, they can better understand why it's a long-term investment worth making. They'll add ceiling fans and flower beds and hardwood floors to their own learning.

They'll own it. Live in it. And they won't want to move out.

ON THE BLOG:
20% PROJECTS:
7 IDEAS TO THINK ABOUT

ON THE BLOG:
BADGES VS. CURIOSITY: WHAT
SHOULD MOTIVATE STUDENTS?

‹Chapter 15›
CHOOSE TO CHEAT

Early in my teaching career, I often wondered if it would be easier to keep a cot in my classroom, since that's where I seemed to live. Between teaching and coaching swimming, there was time for little else. I barely had enough time to get both the teaching and the coaching done!

In a small school district, it's common to teach several different classes. I had four different courses, from two sections of Spanish 1 to a one-student independent study of Spanish 4. As a brand new teacher, the workload made life complicated—especially being newly married. Life got even more interesting when our first daughter arrived.

Every night, I wrote out what I thought was the perfect lesson for the upcoming day. I'd bask in the glow of completing one class's preparation for just a moment before diving into the plans for the second, third, and fourth of the night. I did my best to spend undivided attention on my wife, Melanie, and newborn Cassie. But more often than not, I ended up watching Cassie play while looking over the screen of my laptop computer or with one eye on a lesson plan book.

I could talk about the hours and hours I spent prepping for and coaching swimming for five years, but I think you get the picture. I was busy, and time scarcity made me consider spending some nights at school.

I was cheating on my family... on my life. I didn't plan to cheat. I wasn't trying to cheat, but I did.

We're all cheaters as educators. We cheat every day—every one of us—when we plan, when we grade, when we teach. We cheat. To an extent, we have to because there are only twenty-four hours in the day and one hundred sixty-eight hours in the week. When our list of really good, really important to-do items extends well beyond the slots in our hourly planners or calendar apps, we cheat.

Andy Stanley, senior pastor at Northpoint Community Church in Atlanta, delivered a sermon called "Choosing to Cheat,"[1] that offers an excellent, relevant message regardless of your religious views. I've listened to the recording multiple times and have played it for my wife. (Yes, crazy as it sounds, I played a message called "Choosing to Cheat" for my wife.)

The crux of Stanley's message is the question: "What do you do when your work life is so full you don't have time for the people who matter most?" It's a dilemma all busy people must come to grips with at some point.

For me, the lesson hit hardest when things were going really well in my life. I had taught for few years and was coaching a combined boys-and-girls swim team. We were few and inexperienced, but steadily improving.

One evening after finishing a long Saturday swim meet, I went straight to praise team practice at my church where I played guitar. I hadn't yet seen my two daughters—Cassie had a newborn sister, Hallie—that day. We practiced a little longer than I expected, and as soon as I strummed the final chord on our last song, I quickly packed up and headed out the door. Missing my family, of whom I had seen very little that week, I looked forward to at least a few moments of family time before we all went to bed.

Glancing at the clock in the car I realized just how late it was. I called Melanie to let her know I was done and on my way home. Her response: "OK, but the kids are already asleep."

Asleep. They were asleep. I had missed an entire day—in truth an entire week—of newborn coos and toddler giggles. They were so tiny, and I knew they would grow up in a heartbeat. And they were asleep.

I cried the remaining five minutes of that drive. Then I cried on my wife's shoulder for a few more minutes when I got home.

My swim team was important and worthwhile. My students were creating experiences they would tell stories about to their children. They swam a little faster every week, and I knew my coaching had improved. I loved coaching, and my swim team was starting to become the most important thing in my life. If I'm being completely honest, there's no "starting" to it. At that point in time, the swim team really felt like the most important thing in my life.

But I didn't have enough time to devote to all the important things in my life. So, I cheated. In reality, I had been cheating all along. Instead of staying true to my priorities—God, family, friends, work, and everything else—I had it backwards. I cheated the wrong people. It took years of reorganizing my priorities, but I eventually scaled back my coaching schedule significantly so I could enjoy my family while my children were still young.

All educators must come to grips with a similar question: *What will you do when your teaching life is so full that you don't have time for the work that will have the biggest impact on your students?*

> We have to set aside
> really good, really exciting,
> really useful ideas.
> And that's okay.

I find myself saying this a lot, but it's true: This is an exciting time to be an educator. With so many good tools and materials available, there isn't enough time to try them all.

So we have to cheat. We have to set aside really good, really exciting, really useful ideas. And that's okay. *It's okay to cheat— as long as you keep your priorities in order.* Don't just let it happen, choose to cheat. If you are intentional about it, both you and your students will benefit.

It's hard, I know. As a new teacher, I struggled with this concept of "acceptable cheating." I wanted to try *every* great new idea. My mindset was that I had to grade *everything* my students did. I wanted to teach them *every* important grammar point, vocabulary term, and cultural aspect of Spanish.

I wanted to. And I tried to. But I couldn't. So I started to cheat.

It's hard to go public as a cheater, but I want you to learn from my experience so you, too, can cheat—and reclaim a bit of your personal time.

One way I choose to cheat is to *not* grade everything my students do for me. Grading every activity and every answered question is nearly impossible. Even if I did, there would be diminishing gains on my students' improvement. I may disappoint some educators with this, but grading is a place where some cheating has to happen. So I choose to grade only the most important assignments—the ones that help me check my students' understanding.

Yes, practice assignments are necessary *for them*; but I don't need to grade each one.

Another way I choose to cheat is by looking at differentiating instruction in a new light. At one point in my career, I thought providing individualized learning for each student meant creating lots of different practice activities—reinventing the same lesson over and over, so to speak. It was too time-consuming. These days, I try to reach one or two different learning styles in my class at a time. Teaching this way doesn't reach everyone all at once, but throughout the week, every student's learning style needs are addressed.

Cheating isn't about shirking duties; it's about being extremely intentional with your time. Do the best you can do for your students within school hours and whatever off hours you choose to work. Devote the rest of your time to other worthy causes.

For me, those "causes" are simple: faith, family, and friends. A sign with those three words hangs above a doorway in my living room to remind me every day of the reasons I cheat.

When your life comes to a close, you'll reflect on the most important aspects of your life, the people you love, your relationships, and how you made a difference. Choose to cheat on the things that are less important, and focus on what matters most now. Embrace the right kind of cheating today. You'll be glad you did.

<Chapter 16>
MINIMUM EFFECTIVE DOSE

I know a woman who is a great elementary teacher.
Whenever I want to visit her, I know exactly where to find her: in her classroom.

When I stop by her classroom after school, she's usually seated at her neatly organized desk. She might be grading student projects or homework assignments. She might be filing papers in well-organized, tabbed binders with creative covers, or writing encouraging comments on her students' papers, or preparing innovative activities for her class.

She's a wonderful teacher, and she is very effective. But as I leave her classroom, a question often comes to mind: How much more effective is she than a teacher who spends less time after the final bell rings? Than a teacher who writes fewer comments on student work? Than a teacher whose bulletin boards are less ornate? By the way, don't stop by my class to check out my bulletin boards. They're a disgrace.

I believe, generally speaking, teachers do too much. I know… that sounds like heresy. But hear me out. We arrive before school.

Tiny changes can produce big results, or even the best results.

We stay after school for hours, take work home, create elaborate bulletin boards, and decorate classrooms.

Drive by any school on weekends or holidays and you'll likely see at least a few teachers' cars in the parking lot. These are the same teachers who greet me in the hallway saying, "Boy, it seems like all I ever do is grade papers!" If we're honest, we all feel like that, at times.

Teachers spend hours of their lives—at school and at home—planning, preparing, evaluating, decorating, and grading. Some of the things we do during those extra hours really matter; and some of them don't make much difference at all.

Cutting back to the "minimum effective dose" (MED) could change our lives by helping us optimize our time and resources as educators. The MED is "the smallest dose that will produce the desired outcome," writes Tim Ferriss in *The 4-Hour Workweek.* "Anything beyond the MED is wasteful. To boil water, the MED is 212 degrees Fahrenheit (100 degrees Celsius) at standard air pressure. Boiled is boiled. Higher temperatures will not make it 'more boiled.' Higher temperatures just consume more resources that could be used for something more productive."

In *The 4-Hour Body*, a book that culminated in his "obsessive quest, spanning more than a decade, to hack the human body," Ferris explains how he applies this versatile MED concept to exercise. He writes that he wanted to know, "For all things physical, what are the tiniest changes that produce the biggest results?"

The MED, he discovered, works as well for health as it does for business. Tiny changes can produce big results, or even the best results.

Michael Hyatt uses the minimum effective dose to optimize his blogging time. Hyatt, who writes and speaks about leadership and intentional living, used to publish a new blog post every week-day. He had heard that frequent posts would drive lots of traffic to his website, so he faithfully followed the method. It worked, and he built a huge following of readers who enjoyed his content. Then, Hyatt read an article that claimed the optimal frequency of blog posts was less than daily. It got him thinking: Could he get even better results by publishing fewer blog posts? To find out, he polled his readers. The vast majority of respondents—eighty-one percent—told him they preferred for him to post three times a week or less, not five.[1]

Hyatt's motive was to serve his readers well, but he was pro-ducing more content than his audience could consume. Ultimately, his extra efforts gave him little in return. He immediately cut his posts to two per week. In a podcast interview, he revealed that the traffic to his website—the lifeblood of a full-time blogger—initially shrunk by twenty percent, but it rebounded and grew afterward. The decision gave him more time to produce different, high-quality content including online courses, books, and guest posts for other blogs. In the end, he got more by doing less.

Know When to Stop

What if, as teachers, we could pin down some of those tiny changes? What if we could find ways to cut back and simulta-neously improve our results? How could the MED apply to our careers and classrooms?

Our students are our audience. Much like bloggers, we prepare and present messages. In the end, students will only take in what they feel is necessary to pass a test or to retain for use in life. If we create more content than our audience can consume, it's wasted. Even if the content is interesting and useful, if our students can't absorb it, our efforts are futile. It's like over-boiling water—over-exerting for no extra results.

The truth of MED really hit home when I watched my students pitch corrected papers in the trash. The red-pen technique, which I used liberally, turned out to be a very ineffective way of helping them learn Spanish. Marking all those papers and worksheets consumed hours of my time, and my kids barely looked at my notes before tossing them in the garbage can.

I was over-boiling the water. So I made a change.

Now, my students blog, and I help them through the writing process rather than commenting on their work after the fact. As they write, I circulate around the room, suggest changes, and praise their good work. It's instant feedback. I've learned that working side by side with them, instead of nitpicking their grammar with a red pen afterward, produces better results. They learn more, and I spend less time grading. It's a win-win! Again, it's the least effort to produce the best results—the minimum effective dose. When those blog posts are done, grading them is easy because what they've produced is better.

Teachers often say they're overworked and underpaid, and we are. But maybe the *overworked* part is partially our own fault. By keeping a laser focus on what we want to accomplish, we can reduce or eliminate wasteful and ineffective methods. We can use alternative, less time-consuming, more efficient approaches *and* get better results.

Let's stop over-boiling the water.

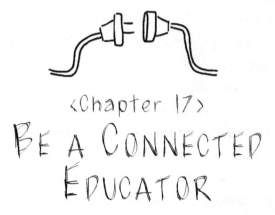

<Chapter 17>

BE A CONNECTED EDUCATOR

I tend to be a lone-wolf teacher.

For years, I alone have comprised the entire world languages department in a very small west-central Indiana public school district. (It makes department meetings really easy.) Before I started connecting with other teachers across the United States and around the world, my "silo" was built up pretty strong. I didn't even realize how self-contained and isolated I'd become, until a keynote speaker showed a picture from the stage and explained that a lot of teachers act like grain silos. (The analogy was easy to understand since I'm surrounded by corn fields.)

To be clear, acting like a silo *isn't* a good thing. Let me explain.

As teachers, we can easily get stuck in our own classrooms—focused on our survival and progress. We build high walls and don't let others enter.

I used to be okay with my own little silo. I've been the only world languages teacher in my district for my entire teaching career. Being the one and only makes it easy to develop the mindset that, "Nobody else understands what I'm doing. I'll just do it alone." But I couldn't do it alone. No one can. The good news is, we don't have to.

First, a wealth of online resources is available to educators today. Can you imagine what teaching was like decades ago? The Internet didn't exist. Filing cabinets stored all the great, and sometimes outdated, ideas. If you wanted to change things up in your classroom, you could innovate on your own, go to a conference for new ideas, buy a book, or visit a colleague. Now there are websites, Twitter feeds, hashtags, and blogs galore. If you want new ideas, all it takes is a simple online search.

Second, other educators are waiting, even eager, to help you, and it's easier than ever before to connect with them. The education community on Twitter grows every week. One Twitter report stated that roughly 4.2 million out of the half-billion tweets every day are about education. That's almost one out of every one hundred tweets! The number of educators who participate in social media is massive. Whatever your question or struggle, you can send out a question via Twitter and get helpful responses, good ideas, and fresh perspectives.

Third, great things are waiting to be done with the power of the aforementioned resources and educators. I met my friend and fellow educator Paula Neidlinger through our state's eLearning community on Twitter (#INeLearn). She teaches junior high humanities (language arts/social studies) at a school a few hours away from mine. Initially, we bounced ideas off each other in our Twitter chats. Then, we decided to team up and present sessions at upcoming educational technology conferences.

Oh—and we hadn't even met in person, yet.

We gathered information in Google documents. We exchanged ideas on Twitter. We crafted a presentation together on Google. Finally, we were ready to present.

And we still hadn't met in person.

Paula and I have now presented multiple times, in person, and have helped other educators find new tools to use in their language classrooms, all because we connected online.

Meeting in person is great, but conferences are infrequent and expensive. In contrast, online educator communities provide you with 24/7 access to people, ideas, resources, philosophies, and opportunities that can expand your world. Here are just a few reasons I've ditched my solo, silo mindset and am so excited about connecting with other educators online.

- **Inspiration:** Ideas abound in online spaces for educators. You'll find new and better ways to teach and the encouragement to try something different.

- **Motivation:** Teachers, by nature, love to motivate. That desire extends beyond the classroom. Educators on social networks can fuel you.

- **Challenge:** A little pushback against your ideas is good. When there are so many philosophies and opinions on education, there's bound to be disagreement. That's okay. It opens your eyes to new possibilities.

- **Camaraderie:** Ever feel alone as a teacher? Hundreds— thousands—of teachers like you are waiting to connect and share in successes and struggles.

- **Apps:** For any task you need to accomplish, chances are there's a digital tool to help you. Teachers who have used those apps can provide direction in choosing the right one for your class.

- **Humor:** We see the funny side of teaching in a way our students don't. It's nice to share our frustrations and joys with people who get us and the realities of the job. Plus, if you can't laugh at your situation sometimes, you might cry.

- **Collaboration:** You can work with virtually anyone anywhere in the world via social networks. Social media makes global connection possible and easy!

So, how much of a time commitment is required to be a *connected educator*? Really, you can decide for yourself. Here are some components of my connected-educator life and how much effort I put into them:

Social media: The easiest connected educator activity to fit in a busy schedule, in my opinion, is Twitter. Each post is 140 characters, so they're quick and easy to fly through. To get quality content in a flash, log in to Twitter (or sign up for an account[1]) and search for #edchat or #edtech. Those hashtags are always full of excellent content. I generally spend anywhere from ten minutes to a couple hours a day on Twitter, totally dependent on how busy my day is and how interested I am in the posted content.

Reading blogs: Thousands of education-related blogs are waiting for your perusal. When you find a few you like, I suggest setting up an account on a free RSS aggregator like Feedly.com and plugging in the web addresses of the blogs you like. RSS readers gather new articles from sites you love so you can see them all in one place. Add lots of blogs to your account that interest you. Every time you log in, it will be like a fresh copy of a personalized, custom-tailored newspaper at your doorstep. You can spend as much time as you want reading blogs each week, from a few minutes to a few hours. I generally spend an hour or two each week reading my favorite blogs.

Writing a blog: I also write articles for my Ditch That Textbook blog. Blogging is a greater time commitment. Each blog post takes me an hour to ninety minutes to write. (The former journalist in me wants to be thorough and to write precisely). However, I know plenty of other bloggers who spend much less time producing their blog posts.

Being a connected educator is the single most important thing I've done to transform how I teach. I have gathered and tried new ideas. I've learned, asked questions, and developed an amazing, online professional learning network. Some days, I can only invest a few minutes. Other days I invest a few hours reading, contributing, and connecting.

My silo walls have broken down, and my teaching has improved as a result. The lone wolf now runs with a powerful pack.

ON THE BLOG:
I JUST CAN'T DO IT ALL: THE CONNECTED EDUCATOR LETDOWN.

<Chapter 18>
SHARE EVERYTHING

"If you create something and don't share it, you're being selfish." That statement from Adam Bellow, the keynote speaker at the 2013 ISTE Conference (the biggest educational technology conference in the world), rattled around in my brain for weeks.

That line—really, the word *selfish*—hit me like a hammer.

The teaching world has changed in the past ten, even five, years. More importantly, the mindset of collecting *my* best ideas and filing them in *my* classroom for *my* use, is slowly being replaced. Today, people like Bellow and so many others, are leading the charge for a more open, collaborative approach to professional development.

Today, access to powerful, free tools helps educators share and gather best practices:

- We can share ideas and discuss them through blogs.

- Conference attendees can distribute powerful quotes, links, and ideas via Twitter and shared digital notes.

- Educators collect their best ideas and publish them in ebooks through Amazon's Kindle, iBooks Author, and PDF downloads.

- Webinars, screencasts, tutorials and speeches can be recorded and uploaded to YouTube.

The one thing teachers can do to make this unprecedented collaborative community *more* powerful is to share.

Share *everything*: ideas, philosophies, practices, and tools.

Share *everywhere*: short messages on Twitter, articles on blogs, full books on Amazon or iBooks Store.

Share in *every medium*: written form, audio (podcasts), and video (screencasts, YouTube).

Share *all the time*: during the school year when you're in the midst of it *and* during the summer when you're recharging and considering the coming school year. Just share.

I can anticipate your concerns.

"I don't understand how this sharing thing works." Pick a medium that fits your style (see the list of tools above) and experiment with it. Twitter is an easy way to get involved. Set up an account, search the #edchat hashtag and start following teachers and sharing ideas you like.

"I don't have anything of value to share." Not true. Every teacher's perspective is different, colored by location, personal experiences, content area, successes, and failures. People love to read about real examples from the classroom. Any teacher can set up a simple blog, describe what works for him or her, post some photos, and share the experience with the world.

"I don't have time to do any of this." Start small. Write a short blog post every week, or every two weeks, about your classroom successes or musings about education in general. Follow a few educators on Twitter and check it for five minutes whenever you get a chance. Record a quick video where you describe and demonstrate your best ideas and upload it.

Ditch the excuses. Just start sharing, *now*. Here are two easy ways to jump in:

Pass your best ideas around with colleagues. As a young teacher, when I returned from a teaching conference, I usually came back inspired to create change in my classroom and in my school. Infused with great ideas and empowered with new resources and exciting tools, those events fired me up to improve my instruction. Know the feeling? If you do, pass it on! Inspiration can be infectious! The idea you share might be the idea that someone needed to see. The best place to start sharing is your own school.

Start a blog. You know, a blog—an online journal where you can post ideas and others can write comments on them. Setting up a free blog on Wordpress.com or Edublogs.org is as easy as signing up for a social media account or new e-mail address. Writing about what you're doing and learning gives you a chance to stop and think. Reflection is a luxury many educators don't afford themselves! Putting your thoughts into words helps you sort ideas out and synthesize them. And when you share them with others in a public forum like a blog, others benefit from your experiences and you benefit from interacting with your readers.

Someone probably shared with you early in your career, and I'll bet it helped you a ton. When I was a first-year teacher, a

Ditch the excuses.
Just start sharing, *now*.

couple of local Spanish teachers let me visit their classes and pick their brains. I stole ideas from them on grading practices, classroom management, and specific teaching ideas. Being a young teacher who didn't have a traditional student-teaching experience in college, I felt as though I'd been left to fend for myself in my classroom. These two teachers were a proverbial rescue helicopter for me on my deserted island.

As I've accumulated more teaching experience, I have worked to remember how I felt in those early years. It's my turn to step up in this cycle of teacher support that goes like this: get help, give help, repeat. Get help, give help, repeat. Create and share, because creating without sharing is selfish.

ON THE BLOG:
CONFESSIONS OF AN
INTROVERT TEACHER

<Chapter 19>

FIND WHAT MAKES THEM TICK

Some teachers seem to easily motivate students while others flounder.

No one wants to scrape by and beg for results. In fact, I bet deep down, most of us want to be motivators like Jaime Escalante. You know, the kind of teacher who persuaded tough, East Los Angeles students to learn calculus and be happy doing it.

While running one day, I heard Daniel Pink interviewed as a guest on NPR's *TED Radio Hour* in a show titled "The Money Paradox."[1] His segment, not surprisingly, focused on money's ability, or lack thereof, to motivate people. Motivation is a huge focus of Pink's work and his TED talk on the subject transformed the way I think about teaching. Aside from all of Sir Ken Robinson's TED talks[2], Pink's "The Puzzle of Motivation"[3] is one of my favorites.

Pink's theory is that carrot-and-stick motivation has a very limited reach. He cites several interesting studies in which incentives produced limited or even negative results. Since rewards and punishment methods so often prove ineffective, he set out to determine what *does* work. How can employers, parents, or teachers effectively motivate the people in their charge? His research reveals that appealing to the much deeper motivations of autonomy, mastery, and purpose is the key. Here's how he defines each of these motivating factors:

- **Autonomy:** "the urge to direct our own lives."

- **Mastery:** "the desire to get better and better at something that matters."

- **Purpose:** "the yearning to do what we do in the service of something larger than ourselves."

Here's how these concepts can motivate students to learn:

Autonomy: Students love the opportunity to choose. Think of a time when you were a student and a teacher chose the mode of learning for you. Perhaps the teacher said, "Work with a partner to... " or maybe the instruction was to, "Sit quietly and read." Chances are one of them made you cringe and the other allowed you to breathe a sigh of relief. You didn't want to be forced into an unappealing method, but traditional, textbook classrooms offered little opportunity for choice. So, you did what you were told.

Ditching textbook mindsets means that we can give students freedom of choice. And as students work in their digital realms in our classrooms, we can motivate them by offering them differing levels of autonomy.

With a goal of *learning* in focus, we are free to choose any number of different digital tools to reach that objective: presentation slide shows, podcasts, video projects, infographics, and websites. With so many ways to demonstrate learning, why pigeonhole students into just one? Sure, it may take a little longer to grade if you're not looking at the same project over and over, but where in modern life is everyone on a team expected to produce the same product?

Mastery: Many of our students are already masters at technology. And that scares us a little bit sometimes. Teachers are so accustomed to being the masters. For decades—*centuries*—we've been the "sage on the stage," imparting wisdom to a captivated (or *captive*) audience.

Acknowledging that students know more than we do about something disrupts the comfortable balance of power teachers have enjoyed for years. But in the information age we live in, anyone can become an expert about anything. It's time to accept that and (from time to time) allow our students be the experts.

For example, a student may be familiar with a new tech tool that could improve learning in the classroom. What if she demonstrated to the class how to use it? Or what if the student learned it herself while she answered questions? The teacher could learn right along with the students.

Let's take it one step further, to a faculty meeting. What if that same student taught other teachers how to use the tool? Think of how empowered that student would feel. Think of the different perspective everyone would gain if professional development was delivered from the student's perspective.

Purpose: Learning for the test has such a limited reach. Passing an exam is not what Daniel Pink meant when he talked about the importance of being part of "something larger than ourselves." Let's put a new spin on education by giving students the opportunity to leverage their learning for something big and important.

I've found that *something* could be as simple as having students practice skills on FreeRice.com. Students answer questions on a number of subjects: different languages, anatomy, chemistry, famous paintings, geography, etc. Every correct answer earns rice for hungry people around the world. The purpose of helping others motivates some students more than simply being told to "study these words."

Or what about a service project? Plenty of worthy local and global nonprofits could benefit from your class's help. Look for ways to connect learning to a charity or identified need. Or find opportunities to use skills learned in the classroom to benefit a cause. When learning has purpose, it takes on a whole new meaning.

Mastery, autonomy, and purpose may well be the fuel your students' engines need.

Another way to look at motivation is with the five C's: choices, challenge, curiosity, cooperation, and competition. I was fortunate to hear college professors Brian Housand of Eastern Carolina University and Angela Housand of University of North Carolina-Wilmington share their insights on the five C's at the National Association for Gifted Children Conference in 2013. While they encourage teachers to reach gifted children with these motivators, they can also inspire just about anyone.

Choices: The Internet provides more choice than we can imagine. In information-gathering, the question becomes: How do we sift through the vast amount of information on the Internet? "We carry in our pockets devices more powerful than what NASA used to put man on the moon," Brian said. We can harness the power to make substantial change.

Challenge: Students are motivated when they are appropriately challenged. If a lesson is "sufficiently challenging," students stay in a state of flow (the correct ratio of challenge to their personal level of skill). Video games utilize this flow state well. If our classes do as well, students will be in the similar state of mind in which they lose track of time, are engaged in the task, and don't notice distractions. Just imagine students so engaged that when the bell rings you hear, "Wow, class is over already?"

Curiosity: We have the unique capacity to attain ever-increasing amounts of knowledge. Episodic curiosity, as Brian explained it, is a cycle more than a line:

- Become curious about something.
- React; do something about it.
- Find resolution in the process, leading to more curiosity.

The cycle is broken when there's too much time between the resolution and the next curiosity.

Cooperation: Feeling part of something bigger than yourself increases intrinsic motivation. Energy develops when students work together with others who have like abilities and interests.

Competition: Friendly rivalry promotes engagement and drive. When the achievement of a group is recognized over individual achievement, the needs for personal recognition can go under-satisfied. Challenging, competitive environments can feed those innate needs.

Do you want to be one of those highly motivational teachers who encourages students on their paths to greatness? Find out which of these motivational elements makes your students tick. Then, create lessons and an environment that inspire them to be their best.

ON THE BLOG:
SIR KEN ROBINSON'S 10 MOST MOTIVATIONAL QUOTES

<Chapter 20>
DON'T DENY THE TECH

Diego Rivera, one of Mexico's most famous artists, got his start as a muralist by—you guessed it—creating art on walls as a child. Instead of punishing him, his parents recognized his gift and empowered him. They covered their walls with chalkboards and canvas, and gave him access to the tools he needed to develop that talent.

In short, his parents didn't take away his paintbrush because he made a mess. Instead, they gave him a place to paint. As an adult, he painted controversial and thought-provoking images on the walls of buildings all over his country and all over the world.

Fast-forward to today's schools. They're filled with smartphones, tablets, computers, apps, and websites. Devices and digital tools are becoming increasingly interconnected with our lives, with our students' lives, and with education. This integration of life and tech begs the question: is technology in schools a privilege or right to students? To be completely honest, this question has left me very conflicted, forcing me to go back to some fundamentals in education and technology.

Education *must* be relevant to our students' future lives. We must prepare them to be contributing members of society. As the saying goes, we're providing them a great disservice if we prepare students for our own future rather than theirs.

Teachers must use the most effective methods available to help students learn. Lecturing often isn't highly engaging or effective. If teachers are going to use the best available tools and methods, lecturing must be cut out as much as possible because it's ineffective.

In light of those fundamentals, the only one conclusion I can reach is: **Technology must be an inalienable right to students.**

In medicine, if a new instrument or technology-assisted procedure improved a surgery by shortening recovery time or reducing the risk of infection, we would *insist* doctors learn to use it. In education, students should be afforded the opportunity to use the tools that will help them learn best. When schools tell students to put cell phones away or limit their access to sites that have valid educational purposes, it's like asking an emergency medical technician to save a life with one hand tied behind his back.

I fully admit this declaration that technology must be a right, not an option, makes part of me cringe. I think about all the time wasted playing mindless games and posting selfies on social media and wonder how we could possibly turn over this easily-abused power to students. Add to this potential for misuse the irritating entitlement attitude so many students have, and my struggle increases.

And then there was the class of high school freshmen and sophomores that really challenged my pro-tech beliefs. It was a full class; I had to add a desk to my room to accommodate everyone. It was also full of big personalities and peer pressure. At times, they broke the teacher I want to be, and led me to incessantly shush

We must be relevant
and use the best tools at
our disposal.

them, yell, assign homework as a punishment, and even cut off
their access to technology.

Yes, the author who just stated that technology is an inalienable right cut off his students' technology. I didn't want to, but
several students were posting inappropriate comments. So I cut
them off for the rest of class that day. Afterwards, we had conversations about the repercussions of their actions. They saw what
life was like without devices and digital learning. After that, I
didn't have to shut them down again.

Sometimes we need to take drastic measures to maintain the
kind of classroom experience our students need—measures like
temporarily banning technology. But I always go back to the fundamentals: We must be relevant *and* use the best tools at our disposal. That means we also have to trust our students *and* teach
them to use technology responsibly. After my class burned me
with technology, I didn't take it away permanently to gain control
or avoid another bad experience. I made clear my expectations
and the consequences, and then I showed my trust by putting that
powerful tool back in their hands. We also tweaked how we used it
to avoid the pitfalls we experienced earlier.

Educators must be free to use the best available tools to teach.
Students should be allowed the same right for learning. This
world is changing quickly, and students need to have access to the
tools that will help them to adapt to it. If we constantly buffer
them from those tools, we're providing them a disservice.

Social media is a perfect example of an experience we need to help our students learn to navigate. School boards and administrators, with their concerns for privacy and security, often remove or restrict all forms of social media. Instead, we should be having conversations about safe, revolutionary methods for integrating social media into the classroom. Social media isn't going away. It's a daily part of life for so many people on the planet and has opened countless doors. Really, it hasn't just opened doors—it has *created* doors that never existed.

A great contribution education can make to today's students is to help them learn how to handle social media safely and effectively *and* to show them the vast potential it holds. It's a lesson that must go beyond the obligatory digital citizenship class. To really learn how to use social media, kids need to use it and see us modeling it. We need to talk with students about what happens online and how they can best use this tool. By sticking their heads in the sand and ignoring or denying the tech, education leaders are missing out on amazing teachable moments.

ON THE BLOG:
11 CLASS ACTIVITIES WITH SENSORS YOU DIDN'T KNOW YOUR PHONE HAD

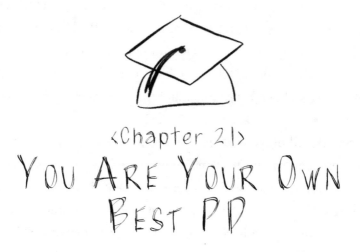

‹Chapter 21›
YOU ARE YOUR OWN BEST PD

"Anyone wanna teach me how to use Twitter? #twitternewbie." That was one of my first Twitter posts. Not very deep, I know. One my first retweets, however, was actually pretty good—and worth repeating here.

The original tweet came from Sean Junkins (@sjunkins), a fabulous technology integration specialist from South Carolina. He wrote: "I've yet to have a student tell me they can't use technology in class because they haven't had any PD on it."

Unlike our students, many educators seem to have an aversion to new technology. Before daring to even consider a new tool, let alone think of a creative, engaging way to incorporate it, these technophobic teachers require an hour of group instruction in front of a computer.

Now, I'm not knocking school-provided professional development (PD). It can give you some valuable skills. And I love how these courses gather teachers in the learning process. But if you're waiting for school-provided PD to answer your every question and guide you on the path of high-quality teaching, you're waiting on the wrong thing.

YOU are your own best professional development. YOU. YOU know your strengths and weakness best. YOU know what you need to capitalize on them. YOU know your true vision of what you want to become. YOU have felt the excitement when the light bulb appears above your students' heads and they "get it." YOU. Not your school's PD coordinator. YOU.

So take all of your strengths, weaknesses, vision, excitement and more, and run with them. Go do some learning. Information, lessons, philosophies, and ideas are all available at the command of a basic Google search or a question sent to colleagues via social media. Never before have so many resources been available, and tomorrow there will be more.

Our students are personal learning gurus, and great role models for us in this regard. Imagine a teenager who gets stuck on a level of Halo or Grand Theft Auto. He has played the same part of the game over and over and has exhausted every idea for beating it.

He doesn't put down the controller and say, "Well, I give up. I guess I'll never see the end of this game." No way! He heads to YouTube and searches for a walk-through video. He texts friends who have played the game and asks them for ideas. Maybe he does a Google search for a discussion board about the game. Honestly, he's probably already a member of multiple discussion boards and doesn't need a Google search to find them.

Hmm... sounds like a good process, doesn't it? Set a vision, find resources to help you realize your vision, and act.

If you're stuck, or simply don't know where to begin with a new-to-you technology, try one of these ideas to jump-start your learning process:

There's a video for that. One of the best ways to learn about a new digital tool, teaching method, or technique is to watch or

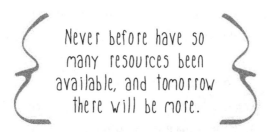

Never before have so many resources been available, and tomorrow there will be more.

listen to someone doing it or explaining it. YouTube and other video sites offer a treasure trove of video tutorials and explanations of new ideas. For example, standards-based grading caught my attention. To learn more about it, I listen to Rick Wormeli's video manifestos.[1] ISTE has also uploaded a ton of presentations[2] on YouTube from its technology conferences on a wide variety of tools and topics.

Ask your students. Not sure what to learn next? Ask some kids. If you are in an administrative role and don't have students of your own, find some to ask. Figure out what interests them, what learning methods work best for them, what they'd be excited to do. Then turn their answer into your next big thing in your classroom or career—even if it makes you uncomfortable (which isn't necessarily a bad thing!).

Check the blogosphere. According to a Blogging.org infographic, 31 million bloggers posted on 42 million blogs as of 2012. A small percentage of those are education blogs, and there are some really good ones. I especially like Spencer Ideas[3] written by John Spencer.[4]

How do you find blogs? Educators constantly share links to their favorite articles on Twitter. An easy way to find great blogs is to do a search for #edchat on Twitter. If you find a blog post you like, you may have found a blog you want to follow. (See page 98.)

Get connected and listen. Thousands of educators are sharing their learning and inspirations through social networks. There are plenty of options:

- **Twitter.com:** probably the busiest education community out there right now.
- **Google Plus** (plus.google.com): one of the fastest growing online communities for educators.
- **Sanderling.io:** a new and growing network created by educators for educators.
- **Pinterest.com:** a very visual option with tons of educational resources.

Choose one—or more!—that fits you best and connect with inspiring educators around the world. Listen to what they have to say, and be brave enough to apply it.

Crowdsource your learning. Once you get connected to other educators through social networks, ask them for ideas about what to learn next. You might be surprised at what they suggest. The saying goes, "The smartest person in the room is the room." So ask the room!

Make it up. Your best ideas might come from analyzing your own situation. Take a good hard look at your students. What motivates them and gets them excited? (Okay, you've probably done that before.) Then, let your creativity flow and create lessons that involve or rely on technology, even if—no, especially if—it's in a way you've never seen it done before. There's a good chance some of your ideas will fall flat. That's all right. Change is difficult.[5] Plus, your students will thank you for trying something new.

Let someone rub you the wrong way. As you get familiar with online education communities, you'll find that many of them ooze with positivity. In many ways, that's a good thing. But if you're not connected to some voices that challenge you or espouse opinions and ideas that go against what you believe, you run the risk of stagnating as a professional. People who are brave enough to challenge others in a professional, productive way are a true asset. Find some and grow with them.

Remember: YOU can set the perfect course for your own improvement. YOU have the power in your own hands.

YOU are the driving force.

YOU are your own best professional development.

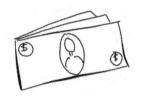

<Chapter 22>

SELL IT TO YOUR STUDENTS

Robert Louis Stevenson said, "Everyone lives by selling something." That goes for teachers, too. Teachers sell motivation. They sell their product, their content. They sell responsibility.

Don't want to consider yourself a salesperson? That's fine, as long as you realize you're acting, thinking, and talking like one anytime you try to persuade people to your way of thinking. Even for teachers who *think* they have complete control over their classes, persuasion is necessary. Just ask education and creativity expert Sir Ken Robinson.

"Nobody else can make anybody else learn anything," he said in a keynote speech at the Music Manifesto State of Play Conference.[1] "You don't make the flowers grow. You don't sit there and stick the petals on and put the leaves on and paint it. You don't do that. The flower grows itself. Your job, if you are any good at it, is to provide the optimum conditions for it to do that, to allow it to grow itself."

We can't make our students learn, so we work to sell them on the value of learning. We sell our students on the benefits of using the last five minutes of class to do homework rather than take a nap. We sell them on the importance of the Pythagorean Theorem and how they'll use it in their lives. We sell, sell, sell, and the best teachers get students to buy, buy, buy.

Selling our students on education is no easy feat. It's a noisy world! Everywhere they look, someone's trying to sell them something. Their focus gets fractured in countless directions—by parents, teachers, after-school activities, social media, video games, and teenage relationships. It doesn't take much to get distracted. When I was a kid, even the cows outside my social studies classroom were difficult to ignore... especially when they started giving us demonstrations of bovine reproduction.

Battling distractions is a difficult task for even the most seasoned salesperson. Unfortunately, most educators have never had any formal sales training—and we have the toughest market! So, how do we break through the noise? How do we convince students to block out the distractions, buy into, and then use what we're selling?

Daniel Pink offers some clues in his book *To Sell Is Human*. Although the book focuses on a career in traditional sales, his message easily translates to teaching. Here are a few classroom sales strategies I've picked up from *To Sell Is Human* that you may want to try, too.

1. Let them tell you why they agree with you. Create the context for students to agree with you, and then get out of the way. Don't force on them your reasons for agreeing. Let them draw conclusions on their own.

As teachers, we make little sales, like getting students to participate in class. We make big sales, like helping them plan for their future. To make your pitch, set the scene and then let students make their own connections between your message and their life. "When people have their own reasons to agree with you, they adhere to them more strongly, believe them more deeply," Pink writes.

2. Decide whether to pitch with facts or questions. We've all made sales pitches to students, colleagues, administrators, and even our loved ones. Through experience, you've probably learned that basic persuasion often involves a series of facts or questions. Pink explains that the effectiveness of any sales pitch is based, at least in part, on the appropriate use of these questions or facts. Here's how you can know which to use:

Make your case with questions if the facts are clearly on your side. Why? Your questions elicit the answers you want to hear. If the answers to your questions are obvious, your questions will lead your subject on the path you want them to take. If they're not, your subject could wander off track.

Make your case with facts when your case isn't open-and-shut. This more restrictive method is your best chance for success if your subject has many plausible choices and you want him or her to select a particular one.

3. Remember that your digital audience is wider than ever. Social media has the potential to magnify what you do in the classroom, be it positive or negative. An exciting learning experience in class may reach other students, teachers, parents, and administrators if your students share it on Facebook or Twitter. That exposure could build interest in your classes and your subject area. A misunderstanding or poorly chosen words could have the opposite effect, though. Pink compares this word-of-mouth exposure to the farmer who sells sweet corn from the back of a truck along the roadside. If he rips off his clients and they tell their friends and family, his business suffers. If he takes good care of them, they tell their friends and business grows.

4. Be a servant leader. The old tried-and-true selling approach of serving people first and then selling to them is still effective. Relationships are key, and good teachers know how to connect. Students are more likely to take advice from adults they see as role models and with whom they have close relationships. It's like the auto repairman who listens to a clanking car on his free time and later sees his business booming with trusting clients.

5. Help people find their needs. In the information age when answers to our questions are only a Google search away, sometimes people don't need answers. They need people who can help them identify their needs. "Identifying new problems is as valuable as solving existing ones," Pink says. Students are often quick to find solutions to their problems. But they need caring adults to help them identify their most pressing problems or evaluate their solutions. As education innovator Carol Ann Tomlinson says, "Students pose two fundamental questions that relate to their motivation to learn: Does the teacher see me? And how does the teacher see me?"

Bringing sales into the classroom might seem a little counterintuitive. But in the end, you're not trying to force students to do something that's only going to benefit you. You're convincing them to act in a way that will potentially empower them for their entire lives. That's the kind of sale I want to make.

FOUR WAYS TO GET STUDENTS' ATTENTION

Michael Hyatt wrote his book *Platform* to help authors, speakers, and leaders "get noticed in a noisy world." He notes that a platform is important for anyone with something to say or sell. That definitely qualifies teachers: We have something to say every day, and we don't want it to fall on deaf ears. Here are some of Hyatt's principles for platform building that apply to teaching:

1. Don't ask for more than you give. Spammers bombard perfect strangers with emails begging them to buy, buy, buy or click, click, click. They are only interested in what they want you to do. They ask without giving.

Teachers ask a lot of students, and rightly so. But whenever possible, give back. Talk to students. Go to their activities. Make them feel important. Reward them with something sugary... that always seems to work.

2. Add value. In platform-building, adding value means considering the audience and giving it something worthwhile. In teaching, it's basically the same. Sure, education is built on the idea of providing valuable content and experiences all the time. But students don't always see the obvious value, especially in today's instant-gratification culture.

Give your students something they can use today. Something they want today: a fascinating news blurb, a relevant joke, something sugary. (Wait, haven't we touched on that already?)

3. Write shorter posts, shorter paragraphs, and shorter sentences. Teachers may not write for students like bloggers write for audiences, but we do present content in a similar way. Content overload prevails in today's always-on culture. Don't add to the problem. If a four-minute explanation works as well as a fifteen-minute discourse, why go on for fifteen minutes? Think KISS: keep it simple, stupid. In the words of Rusty from the movie *Ocean's Eleven*, "Don't use seven words when four will do."

4. Engage in the conversation. Hyatt notes that building a platform requires interacting with followers. People want a personal connection. To fulfill that desire, you've got to reach out, be real, and participate in two-way conversations. Similarly, students don't just want to hear you lecture. Be yourself. Tell them your stories. Connect with them. Engage. And while you're talking with them, why not hand them something sugary? (It always comes back to sweets!)

On the Blog:
Why "Holes in Wood" Beat "Drills" in Education

SECTION 3

DITCH THAT TEXTBOOK

What's working in your classroom?

What isn't working?

What would you like to improve?

What would you like to toss out altogether?

Ditching your textbooks means looking for different, innovative, tech-laden, creative, and hands-on ways of teaching. As you evaluate your current methods, you may discover some areas in which your class really shines. And you may also find gaping holes that you need to fill with customized content.

In this section, we'll look at some of the practicalities of creating a relevant, digitally enhanced classroom. If you like the idea of going paperless and incorporating technology into your lessons but are wondering how to do it, you're going to love what's coming up next.

<Chapter 23>

CREATE A HOME FOR YOUR STUFF

When I ditched my textbooks, the Web became our new, somewhat messy home. I directed my students to numerous websites. In our paperless classroom, they created content using all sorts of digital tools. Documents I created got mixed in with student assignments submitted to me. It was an organizational nightmare! The more online resources I added to the mix, the more I realized I needed a home base—a simple website for my classes—where I could keep materials for future reference.

But I wasn't interested in the static websites I'd seen for other classes. I wanted something that did more than simply presented information about the class and the teacher, and maybe offered a syllabus. I'd seen sites like that. They felt stale and, honestly, they didn't get much traffic on the Internet because they weren't relevant to the students or anyone else.

I wanted to create a home base for my classes that was dynamic, eye-catching, and relevant to my students. It would have resources essential to progressing in the course. I didn't want to have to write HTML, Java, or another coding language, nor did I want a programmer as a website gatekeeper. Until recent years, those barriers prevented many people from creating an online presence.

I chose Weebly.com, an easy-to-use online tool for building websites, to create my class site. I like Weebly because the education version comes through our district's Internet filter with no problems. I also really like its drag-and-drop options. Other options exist for creating free websites, such as Google Sites and Wikispaces. I just prefer Weebly's user-friendly interface.

Getting started was simple. I simply set up an account, just as you would with e-mail or social media, added pages, and then filled my site with content. Links to Google Docs and flashy embedded content, like interactive online flash cards and YouTube videos, make it interactive and useful for my students. It's possible to create individual pages within a site, so I have a separate page for each class as well as a page that includes a list of websites used by all my classes. Each page can be named and listed in a clickable menu for easy access.

Tons of content can be integrated to your class page and your class website by posting links on your site. Here are a few ideas:

1. Documents. By creating your documents on Google Docs, or uploading your old documents to your Google Drive account, you can generate a link to them. Post those links on your class website and you'll never have to dig out photocopies for your students again.

2. Tests and quizzes. I often create tests and quizzes using Google Forms and then post a link to them on the class site. When students are finished with the test or quiz, I remove the link immediately or turn off submissions to the form.

3. Embedded videos. Numerous educational videos are available on YouTube (or SchoolTube or TeacherTube) to help teach the Spanish grammatical concepts I'm introducing in class. Take a look and see what resources relate to your area of instruction. You may be surprised at the quantity and quality of videos available. Giving students access to these videos reinforces the lesson and provides an easy reference for absentees. Note: Videos don't take the place of instruction. As their teacher, I'm still the one who best understands the needs of my students; videos supplement my carefully planned curriculum.

4. Quizlet flashcards. I'm a huge fan of Quizlet.com, an online flashcard site. After quickly creating a set of Quizlet flashcards, you can embed an interactive version on your site. Students can then flip through terms without having to leave.

5. Images of student work. My students create a lot of content for me—drawings, comic strips, etc.—and sometimes we create illustrations for our Spanish stories together. Posting these images on the class website provides a fun way to refer back to what we've done together and to jog students' memories about what they've learned.

6. Photos of students. Students engage in lots of exciting, visually appealing activities during their years in school. Capture those moments with digital photos and include them on your class

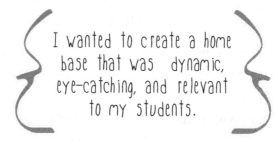

I wanted to create a home base that was dynamic, eye-catching, and relevant to my students.

website. Students will feel more at home on your site, and they'll have more reasons to visit it if it is updated regularly with new content. Note: Make sure to follow your school's procedure for posting photos of students.

7. Your contact information. Want to make it easy for students to contact you? Create a link to your e-mail address and include a contact form where students type their name and question and send it to you via the site. Adding SpeakPipe to your site allows students to leave you a voice message and will send you an e-mail notification when they do.

8. News you can use. Include an RSS feed, a clickable stream of news or articles, on a widget (a small, customized program embedded on a web page) or use RSSinclude. Students will instantly be able to see new articles on your site that might interest them.

9. Sub lesson plans. Cynthia Basham, a world language teacher from Evansville, Indiana, leaves lesson plans for substitute teachers, using tools like Screencast-O-Matic or Screenr to record a video of her computer screen and her voice. Instead of, or in addition to, written lesson plans for a substitute teacher, you can avoid misunderstandings or miscommunication by creating a video explaining what to do—in your own voice, no less!

10. A poll. Students want to hear their own voices in your class! Ask them for their opinions by linking to or embedding a poll using Google Forms, Poll Everywhere, or Mentimeter. Then actually do something with their results to make it count!

11. Something about you. Students love to know more about the real lives of their teachers. Include an "About Me" page with photos, links to things you like, and information about your background. Write about topics they'd expect, but surprise them, too!

12. Some competition. ClassBadges is a tool that allows you to create badges to recognize students for their work and link it to your site. Video gamers and athletes crave this kind of recognition and other students do, too. My students also love the leaderboard on Quizlet. They race each other in the learning games to see who comes out on top!

13. A teacher blog. Blogging is a great way to provide information and share the wonderful things happening in your class. Many site-creation tools like Weebly offer a blog option. There are many benefits of starting a teacher blog,[2] and your students will love it!

14. Student blogs. If you can blog, so can your students! Offer a single blog where your students can contribute either as an assignment or voluntarily, or host individual student blogs on the class site. If you prefer a separate site for blogging (my favorite is KidBlog), links can make it easy to share and highlight students.

You don't need tons of content on your class website to get started. I begin each school year with a clean slate, archiving the previous year's content and adding new links and content as students need it. The beauty of creating a website is that it can be shaped to fit your needs and updated quickly. Start small and add to it at your own pace!

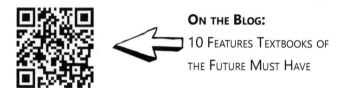

ON THE BLOG:
10 FEATURES TEXTBOOKS OF THE FUTURE MUST HAVE

<Chapter 24>
CREATE CONTENT

One thing textbooks are great for is delivering content. So once you ditch your textbooks, you'll need another resource for material. My suggestion: Create content yourself.

Since the first year I decided to rely less on textbooks, I've delivered much of my content via study guides that showed students what they were accountable for learning each week. The advantages to this approach are huge! My study guides are customizable; I don't have to stick with the vocabulary or sequence of topics in the textbook. As long as I meet academic standards and school requirements, I can tailor the content to my students' needs. Textbooks, on the other hand, may as well be set in stone.

I started with photocopied Word documents, which were fairly easy to modify even after they were copied and distributed. Just apply the low-tech, student pencil-to-paper technique. When I switched to Google Apps for Education, I transferred those study guides to Google Docs and shared them with students as links on our class website.

Teacher and student-created documents are just the tip of the online content iceberg! Countless resources can be created online to support student learning. Here's an A-to-Z list of ideas you can start plugging into your classes immediately!

Audio Essays: Give students a chance to state their case. Audio essays—whether the thirty-second or multiple-minute variety—let students inform and persuade verbally, a skill they will need in the workforce. Record their essays using Google Voice's digital voicemail.

Blogs: Turn student writing into a digital and collaborative activity. Students publish blog posts and classmates read others' work and add comments.

Choose Your Own Adventure Stories: Remember the books that allowed you to choose what happened to the main character simply by turning to a certain page? Students can create similar stories in Google Forms. Set up the story for your students and then have them each write an alternate ending, or a portion of a story.[1] Using links, the readers can click on and read different stories based on their choices.

Debates: Debates take interviews to the next level. Students select a topic and can join with one or more classmates to record their discussion using a Google Hangout on Air or an audio recording on AudioBoom.com. The recorded debate can then be shared with the class.

Earth Tour: Google Earth is good for more than checking out what your house looks like from outer space. Students or teachers can place pins in various geographic locations and then jump from place to place with the class or individually for a quick visual tour.

Future Predictions: Based on what they've learned, let students tell you what they think the future will be like. Using Creative Commons photos, icons, and text, they can draw or use an infographic creation tool, like Piktochart, to create visual predictions.

Galleries of Art: Gathering examples of great artwork created by professional artists or student artists has never been easier. Students can collect digital photos, scans, or even digitally-created artwork and then share them with others via a slideshow, blog, or web page.

House Plans: Online home-designing tools such as Floorplanner let students design floor plans for houses. Students can create a floor plan for a historical building and label it with new vocabulary terms, or connect their design skills with other content areas such as book summaries or lab reports.

Interviews: Students can take interviews in so many directions. For example, they can ask friends' opinions about class-related topics, interview family members to delve into their own genealogy, or talk with community experts about a research topic. Have them record their interviews with video or audio using free, online tools such as Google Hangout, Google Voice, or AudioBoom.

Judgment Evaluations: Students can put their digital-citizenship skills to work by finding examples of errors in judgment or examples of good judgment in other online sites. Create an online poster using Smore or Google Drawings to explain their views on why a decision was good or bad.

Kinesthetic Learning: Get students out of their chairs! Students can use tablets and other touch-based devices to gather photos and video. The Move It extension for Google Chrome suggests quick physical activities students can do to break out of their sedentary habits. Both a change of scenery and getting the blood pumping can make a positive difference in the classroom.

Logs for Nutrition and/or Exercise: Online survey tools like Google Forms make a great resource for collecting information about students' nutrition and exercise habits. Create the survey and share it with students. Their responses will be collected in a spreadsheet and can be analyzed. Note: Be sure to add a text field to collect students' names.

Messages by Video: Video sharing sites (YouTube, TeacherTube, or Vimeo) and video chat services (Skype or Google Hangout) allow students to record visual responses to common questions or prompts. Create short videos and share with a link. Connect with another class and share video messages using the video chat services.

Natural Science Documentation: Digital photos and videos are excellent ways to log the weather, growth of plants, and changes in animals. Share that digital media by publishing it on a website. Connect with a class in another part of the country, or world, to compare results.

Online Music Recitals: Audio creation tools, like Audacity and GarageBand, empower students to make digital versions of their music. Upload student compositions to an audio host like AudioBoom to give student performances a global audience.

Presentations (Shared): For an easy-to-set-up collaborative activity, share a slideshow using Google Slides or a PowerPoint using Microsoft 365. Assign each student a slide to fill with class-related content. Within minutes, they can create a large, far-reaching resource everyone can benefit from.

> I don't have to stick with the topics in the textbook.... I can tailor the content to my students' needs.

QR Codes: Often used to direct your device to a website, these psychedelic bar codes can also direct students to content via a link or even deliver short messages. Create QR codes using free online tools. (Just search for "create QR codes" in a search engine.) Post QR codes around the classroom and school and encourage students to include them in projects to give a new dimension of information for their audience.

Raps, Songs, and Chants: Adding music or a beat to words can be a powerful memory device. Years later, my former students can recall songs and chants they used to learn countries, capitals, and the days of the week in Spanish. Video and audio creation tools like WeVideo, Audacity, and AudioBoom, let students share their memory devices with others.

Screencast Videos: Teachers and students can create videos that display their screens. They can use those videos to demonstrate key information or processes. Share access to these videos so others in the school, and beyond, can benefit as well.

Talk Shows: Want to provide an engaging format for delivering instruction or showing student learning? Create talk shows (aka podcasts) either in person or by piecing together audio from different students. They're easy to digest, especially if students listen to them "on the go" from their portable devices. Podcasts can tackle topics in a fun and creative way. Use a simple online audio tool like AudioBoom to capture the audio and share it.

Unbelievably Easy Animated Videos: PowToon, and similar tools, can help you and your students create animated videos and design engaging, fun videos with moving parts, sliding text and music. These videos can be used to demonstrate understanding and teach others creatively!

Visual Notes and Organizers: Using online drawing tools (Pixlr or Google Drawings) or art apps on touch-based devices (Paper or whiteboard apps) enable you to pull ideas together visually. The Picture Superiority Effect asserts that pictures, even bad pictures, have a drastically higher impact in presentations than words alone. Let's put that power to work in the classroom! To learn more about graphic organizers you can add to your class, check out my blog post: "15 Free Google Drawings Graphic Organizers."[2]

Whiteboard Animation Videos: Entertaining and engaging, these videos in which an arm furiously scribbles drawings on a whiteboard are easy to create. Simply record the video at regular speed, use a video editing program to speed it up, and record a voice over the top of it. They're a powerful way to deliver content.

"Xtreme" Movie Posters: Using the drawing and creation tools mentioned earlier, students can create movie posters, complete with a large image, title, and tagline. Adding digital elements with QR codes or Aurasma auras (i.e., video and image layers that appear over the poster on a device screen) make it *extreme!*

Young Authors: Publishing platforms, such as comic strip-creation tools (Make Beliefs Comix or Pixton) and digital storytelling tools like StoryBird empower student authors. Students can create their own ebooks and even list them on booksellers' websites like Amazon and Barnes & Noble.

Zany Talking-Head Videos: Talking avatar videos (Chatterpix or Voki) can give a fun voice to content. For example, upload a picture of Abraham Lincoln and let him share his opinions. Use historical lessons to hypothesize what he might say about current problems. Give him a crazy hair-do and other props, and try to mimic his voice to add humor.

An overarching feature of content created online is the option to share it. Content created in traditional ways—on paper, poster board or on a chalkboard—gets trapped in the classroom. Expressing ideas digitally makes it easy to share them all over the world. Your classroom can have a global reach!

‹Chapter 25›
WRITE, READ, AND SHARE

My students love to tweet and share photos on Instagram. As expert digital collaborators, they are aware of all the cool, viral YouTube and Vine videos. They spend hours discussing topics near and dear to their hearts on social media. Theirs is an online world, and I want my content to be a part of the world they love.

Tapping into that world has never been easier. One of my favorite ways to engage with students online is through their blogs. Writing blog posts opens up students to all kinds of interaction. In this personal space on the Web, they can publish posts and receive comments from anyone.

Blogs have the potential for a worldwide audience. Before this current technology, students usually wrote for an audience of one: the teacher. Their multi-page compositions were put in the teacher's inbox to be graded. When they got their papers back, they were marked with red ink… and only one person had read it. Even if their audience grew because their papers were passed around the classroom for other students to read, it was still limited.

These days, blogs, and other forms of writing online, can lead to easy, meaningful collaboration and a significantly larger audience. Student writing no longer has to be confined to the eyes of the teacher. As a class, students can easily read one another's work and engage with it by adding comments and participating in comment conversations. But that's only the beginning. Public blogging gives students a potential audience of *millions* of readers. Social media and Comments 4 Kids[1], a program to give student work some global interaction, further increase the potential reach of student work. The impact is similar to giving elementary students an audience for their Christmas program. At practice, the students might goof off or be inattentive. But give them an audience at the program and they nail it every time.

Writing for such an expansive audience is one of those activities that could never happen without technology. It's *redefinition*, the "R" in the SAMR model for using technology. (See page 72.) Think of the implications of publishing your writing and sharing it freely with (potentially) millions of people around the world.

What would that look like without modern technology? The low-tech alternative would be writing something, photocopying it (which actually adds a bit of technology), and mailing thousands of copies around the world. That's a lot of folding letters, licking envelopes, and spending hundreds of dollars, if not thousands, on postage. Blogging is free and instantaneous.

So, let's say you're convinced of the benefits of blogging. What should students write about? Topics can be as varied as the students, the teacher, and their philosophies. Here are some ideas:

Write about Class Content and More: Connections to and opinions about class content are great, especially if students discuss via comments. But we're missing a great opportunity if we limit topics to their studies. Blogs give kids an opportunity to reflect on their lives and what's important to them, something they don't automatically do.

Open Topic Posts are Good: Students could reflect on what they've learned that week in a simple blog post. The blog could be open to all classes or just your content area.

Go to the Students' World: Meet students in their world as much as possible. Making content touch their lives creates a connection that can last a lifetime. Listen to what they talk about in class—pop culture, music, sports, etc.—and have them write about that. Or ask them to write about a personal relationship that mirrors the relationship of two characters from that novel your class is reading.

Let Students Pick: Ask students for writing prompt suggestions. You might be surprised by the creative, relevant connections they make.

Once topics are selected, it's time for students to roll up their sleeves and start writing. Here are some ideas for creating blog posts:

Teamwork Works: Encourage students to connect with each other in their posts to make them more personal, but not just in the comments they leave. Q&A interviews and polls work well. You can also incorporate teamwork by having students pair up for blog post assignments. That blinking cursor on a new blog post may seem less daunting if students don't have to confront it all alone.

Do Your Homework: Encourage or require students to link facts used in their posts to real-world sources. Link web pages. Cite hard copy texts. Use direct quotes when citing a classmate's opinion. Professional bloggers do this. Why should student bloggers be different?

Encourage Readability: Good blog writing crosses over from the real world to the classroom. Internet content is written for people with short attention spans. Good bloggers know that their messages can easily be drowned out by the noise of incessant marketing. Catchy introductions, a "what's it about" paragraph early on, bullet points and lists, short paragraphs, simple sentences, and conclusions with questions are the norm. If that's not the kind of writing you want your students doing, that's okay. Some teachers use blogs for formal essays. Others use them for conversation with posts and comments as short as text messages. Blogs can be whatever you want them to be.

Reward Out-of-Class Blogging: Creating a blog culture that makes students want to continue blogging outside the classroom is powerful. If students own their blogs and take responsibility for them, they'll create great content and keep writing, which is the goal! Try incentives for after-hours blogging (e.g., extra points or privileges, polls or games for interest, etc.). Encouraging blog responses to current events (e.g., school activities, news, etc.) gives students even more ideas for what to blog about at home.

Give Them Plenty of Time: Rushing students to write and comment leads to shallow content. A blogger myself, I know my best content comes when I start formulating an idea days before I actually write the post. When I sit down to write, I'm not pulling ideas out of thin air. Allowing a little time can encourage great digital conversation.

Emphasize Clean Copy: Blogs don't usually follow text-message writing convention. Unless you address that point, some students might miss it. Solid spelling, correct grammar, and idea development gives students credibility in their readers' eyes.

But Don't Nitpick: I have worked hard to avoid the temptation to correct every spelling and grammar error. In foreign language teaching, as in many other disciplines, teachers get caught up in highlighting mistakes in red ink instead of encouraging great topic development and writing. Real-life blog readers rarely nitpick grammar. Plus, constant criticism can discourage students' creativity and initiative. If a poor spelling or grammar pattern emerges, consider addressing it privately.

Once the posts are written, the process is finished, right? No way! This is only the beginning of the digital conversation. Here's what to do after students click PUBLISH:

Make Quality Comments: Well-thought-out comments are like jewels and add value to online conversation. They supplement ideas and information, share personal experiences, provide insightful links and quotes, and ask follow-up questions. Unfortunately, writing quality comments is not intuitive for kids. Without a bit of instruction, you may end up reading shallow responses, one-word comments, or, worse, one-letter comments like "K"!

Choose a Stance on Comments: Comments for student blogs seem to fall into two schools of thought: quantitative and qualitative. The *quantitative stance* has countable requirements such as: students write three comments, forty words, etc. It assures participation and makes grading easy. However, it also promotes an "I have to" mentality that fails to bring out the best conversations.

The *qualitative stance* values quality of discussion over quantity. Teachers may develop a rubric that shows students how they should comment but doesn't specify how many comments and words are required. This approach may result in less participation, though, as some students may see a lack of specific requirements as a license to do less. A combination of quantitative and qualitative may be the best option for encouraging quality discussions in blog comments.

Create Respect: The lack of face-to-face communication in online discussions makes it easy for students to forget that real people—their peers—actually read what they write. Students can become brazen and post harsh comments and forget that civility should rule in all our conversations.

High-Five Good Work: Find ways to promote quality blog posts and comments outside of the student blog. Mention or post them in class, add them to the class website, or include them in school newsletters.

Decide on Privacy: Some of the most spirited debates in conference sessions I lead are about whether to make student blogs public or private. Public student blogs offer an authentic, global audience but potentially expose kids to the harshness and dangers of the real world. Students thrive on comments from the outside world. Thankfully, you can encourage comments and keep your students safe. One way to give student bloggers a worldwide audience is to post links to student posts on Twitter with the #comments4kids hashtag. Additionally, you can post links to student work on your school's Facebook page or send links through e-mail newsletters to parents. A great way to protect students and eliminate some negative experiences is to require approval for all comments, with you as the administrator who approves or rejects comments.

Break the Economic Barrier: Students without home Internet access, like many in my own lower-income, rural school district,

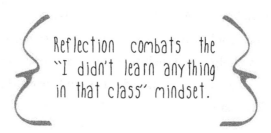

Reflection combats the "I didn't learn anything in that class" mindset.

are at a disadvantage. To combat this, teachers can help students find Internet time during school (e.g., study hall, library time, computer lab time, before and after school). They can also educate them about out-of-school options such as the public library, a friend's house, etc.

Re-Purpose Content with a Cumulative Product: Encourage or assign an end-of-the-year product students can create from their blog posts. They could publish a printed book or a PDF ebook, derive a Weebly website, or compile a "Top 10" list of posts or comments.

Review and Reflect: When students review their work for the year, they see how they've grown... as a writer, a learner, and a person. Reflection reinforces important lessons and combats the "I didn't learn anything in that class" mindset.

Create an Online Home for Student Work: I've really struggled with the concept of handing papers back to my students for a long time. I hate seeing them give them a cursory glance and then pitch them in the trash on the way out the door. Or seeing stray papers end up on the hallway floor or sticking out of the bottom of lockers. Creating online portfolios is a great way to manage student-created content and provide a place to demonstrate students' abilities to others.

Sharing student ideas and work online exposes them to perspectives from people they would otherwise never meet. Those perspectives can help shape their worldview and understanding of other cultures. And as they learn, discuss, and grow, they become better global citizens.

ON THE BLOG:
20 COLLABORATIVE GOOGLE APPS ACTIVITIES FOR SCHOOLS

ON THE BLOG:
20 IDEAS FOR SOLID STUDENT BLOGGING

⟨Chapter 26⟩
Go Global

Do you remember what it felt like to receive a letter from a pen pal? It was electrifying, like a connection from another world! New worlds opened up to students for the cost of postage. Pen pal letters inspired students to learn about other cultures and travel to countries they would never dream of visiting otherwise.

Pen pal correspondence had its drawbacks, though: students might never get a return letter or may be unable to stick with it. In my opinion, the fatal flaw of pen pals is the "pen" which necessitates delayed gratification, a system of communication most people can't tolerate anymore.

These days, there's no reason to wait. With an Internet connection and a device, instant global communication and collaboration is at our fingertips. We can connect with others around the globe through video and text chats, recorded audio and video messages, shared documents, and more.

Going global is one of the most transformative effects the Internet can have on a classroom. Students get front row seats to the rest of the world, putting real faces on facts from geography, science, and language classes. My Spanish 3 class experienced the benefits of global interaction firsthand. For several weeks, I partnered with an English teacher in Valencia, Spain, to plan ideas for shared activities. Then, one day, giving very little direction to my students, I took them to the large-group instruction room at our school. You should have seen the bewildered looks on their faces. It was fantastic!

After a short briefing that included participation guidelines, we were ready to conduct a Mystery Location Call. This activity brings together two classes via video chat using Skype, Google Hangouts, FaceTime or another video chat provider. Other than knowing the other class was in a different country, neither class had any idea where the other was located. The mystery added excitement to that previous bewilderment and created an electric atmosphere! The goal was to discover where the other class was located. Students asked each other Yes or No questions: my students asking questions in Spanish and the Spanish students asking in English. Think of it as a combination of Twenty Questions and Battleship.

To keep students focused, each was assigned a specific job in the process of asking and answering questions. Some remained on camera to ask and answer questions while others used maps and clues from the other class to help narrow down the questions and determine the other class's location. The activity could have stopped after each class guessed the other's location, but the students kept talking. They asked additional questions about the geography of their country and their lives based on their own curiosity.

While this activity produced a great day of connecting and learning, we were only getting started. My students made weekly

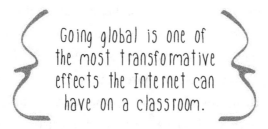

Going global is one of the most transformative effects the Internet can have on a classroom.

Skype calls to the students from Spain, asking and answering questions about assigned topics and topics of their choice. They also collaborated throughout the week in shared Google Docs. Occasionally, one of my students would open a Google Doc and find a Spanish counterpart still typing in the document. Thousands of miles apart, they could see each other formulating ideas on the digital page. Such collaboration could never exist without technology.

Student interactions were one of the best parts of this collaboration. The initial chats were highlighted by technical glitches and the awkwardness that comes with different languages and new faces. But after the first couple of chats, the students started to develop relationships. The same pairs of students from each class met together each week so they got to know one another fairly well. When they were done with their questions for the day, I enjoyed listening to them giggle and chat as friends. One winter day, some of my students showed the students in Spain the heavy covering of snow we had that week. Most of the students from Valencia had never seen snow, especially the kind of deep snow we get in Indiana in the dead of winter!

Some might claim this "silliness" is less than academic, but I disagree. My students discovered a valuable lesson that's often tough to learn in the middle of Indiana cornfields: people are people regardless of where they live. My students found that teenagers from Spain liked the same things they did: to laugh, to look good, to be liked by their friends. They spoke a different native language, but with some work to break down the language barrier, they found many more similarities than differences. Many of my students will never experience international travel so this experience may be their only glimpse at another culture, and I'm thankful it was positive. With so many people in our little agrarian community who refuse to relate to people who are different, perhaps this experience will be a small positive step toward breaking down unfounded fears.

Global connections naturally fit in my world language classroom. But, global activities can be incorporated into almost any class. Class presentations, literature discussions, science labs, exercise regimens, music recitals, problem solving, and visits from authors and experts are just a few activities in which tech tools could expand your students' world.

If you're wondering how to connect, start by getting a Skype or Google account. (Google Hangouts are part of the Google Plus feature of a standard Google account.) Although these two tools are often mentioned at conferences and training as valuable resources, I'm surprised by how few educators actually use them. When I reached out on social media to invite educators to partner with my classes, I received only a few responses. I believe this lack of participation likely stems from three common, but surmountable, stumbling blocks in educational technology:

Anxiety: Fear of the unknown can be paralyzing. Teachers stall out wondering:

What will happen?
How will my students react?
Will they be engaged or bored?
Will it blow up in my face?
How will students view me as a teacher afterward?

The best way to put that fear to rest is to confront it in a safe environment, perhaps initially connecting with another class in your district or school. The reality is, even if an activity doesn't go exactly as planned, global connections will be a positive experience for everyone involved. Your students will be involved in something new and exciting, the other class will get a glimpse of life in your classroom and your area of the world, and you will likely spark new enthusiasm and engagement in your classroom.

Perceived Lack of Technical Ability: Video chats are easy to set up; expert technical skill isn't needed. Simply connect a camera, set up an account on the service you want to use, and connect the account of your partnering class to yours. If the other teacher has done video chats before, he or she may be able to offer some guidance. As with most apps or sites, there's very little you can do to mess up a Skype call or Google Hangout.

Lack of Time: Busyness is an easy excuse for not trying something new. In reality, we make time for what we want to do. I learned what I needed to know about video chatting in less than a weekend, so I know that lack of time isn't the real issue. If we want to make a difference in our students' lives and provide them with unique opportunities, we'll make it happen.

How to Connect

Video chats are my favorite way to make global connections; however, they're only one option for conversing with a class or individual on the other side of the world. For example, you can send video messages using Skype or YouTube if a real-time call isn't possible. Use Voxer to send an instant audio message. Connect in written form with shared Google Docs or exchange messages with ePals, online pen pals. Create an academic, social hub online with Edmodo. Start with whatever means you're comfortable using. Just start!

As you set up your activities, consider the following.

- **Think about time zones.** We have two time zones in Indiana, so even in-state calls are complicated! A simple online search for the time in your targeted location should clear up any time zone questions. Since not all countries change for daylight saving time simultaneously, double check the time with the teacher with whom you'll be collaborating.

- **Be flexible and understanding with the other class.** This is especially important with international calls. Social norms, communication customs, sense of time, and connection issues may be very different. Factors out of everyone's control pop up as well. For example, school day delays and cancellations due to winter weather alter my Skype plans on a regular basis.

- **Talk to students about the experience.** Ask your students what they like about video chatting, what they don't like, what changes they'd suggest and what topics they want to discuss. Then do your best to incorporate their ideas. Students have to be dedicated to the process to make it worthwhile.

Adding some global connections definitely enriched the learning in my classroom. My students have a different view of people from other countries, and they've seen how the Spanish language they've learned in my class can be used in the real world with people their own age. Plus, they had a lot of fun!

Mystery Location Calls

Engaging in a mystery location call with Skype, Google Hangout, FaceTime, or other video chat service is simple and powerful. The goal is for two classes to pair up via video chat and guess where in the world the other class is. Here are the basic steps:

1. **Find another person or class to chat with.** See the "How to Find Other Classes" section in this chapter for resources on connecting with other classes around the world.

2. **Determine the format of the mystery location call.** Yes or no questions are typically used to narrow down the opposing class's general location. Some classes like to try to guess the country, while others choose to be more specific, narrowing down to the state, province, territory, or even the city.

3. **Swap account details and do a test call.** Making sure video and audio work well ahead of time can minimize delays and maximize benefits.

4. **Set a time to connect and don't forget about time zones!** Ensure that 10 a.m. means the same thing to each of you.

5. **Teach your students about mystery location calls.** Brief them about the process, what to do and not to do, and what their jobs will be. Assigning jobs (see the list below) can keep students engaged and on task.

6. **Make the call and have fun!** Consider allowing your students—regardless of age—to run the call as much as possible. Teach them what they'll need to do and offer support if necessary.

Mystery Location Jobs

If students are assigned specific jobs during the call, they'll likely be more engaged during the call. The following is a list of jobs I use for my Spanish classes which can be adapted and revised to fit your needs. My own Mystery Skype job list is an adaptation of lists compiled by Pernille Ripp and JoAnn Fox.[1]

- **Question Askers and Answerers:** One to three students in front of the camera interact with the other class. Others can rotate in if necessary.

- **Mappers:** Two students use maps, either physical or digital on iPads or computers, to guess the location or formulate new questions.

- **Think Tank:** These students process incoming information and help develop questions or guess the location.

- **Question Writers:** Two students formulate the next question in Spanish and write it on a small dry erase board to display to the other class.

- **Grammar Checkers:** One or two students check the accuracy of the Spanish in the question.

- **Word Referencer:** One student uses WordReference.com to look up Spanish words the group doesn't know.

- **Photographer or Videographer:** A student takes photos or video of the activity to post later on our class website.

How to Find Other Classes

Classes, experts, and lots of other people are waiting to teach and learn with your class! Here are some great places to connect with others globally:

Skype Education (education.skype.com): Teachers and others can submit "lessons"—requests to connect educationally via Skype—on the Skype Education site. It's a great place to find people and ideas. Scan through the lessons for someone to connect with or submit your own ideas.

Mystery Skype (education.skype.com/mysteryskype): If you're looking to participate in a Mystery Skype activity, this is a great place to start.

Social Media: Twitter (twitter.com) and Google Plus (plus.google.com) are excellent places to find video chat partners. Search various communities and groups on Twitter, Facebook, and Google. On Twitter, use the hashtag #mysteryskype to connect other with educators who are in search of a class with which to partner. Google Plus has an active community called Mystery Location Calls where educators post requests to connect their classes. I have had success finding educational partners on both.

Colleagues, Family, and Friends: Utilize people you know personally. Ask others to refer you to someone you could connect with. Ask your students, too!

ON THE BLOG:
MORE RESOURCES
TO GO GLOBAL

‹Chapter 27›
MANAGE YOUR CLASSROOM

Having a classroom full of computers at my disposal creates countless opportunities for students to get distracted and lose productivity. I see ESPN and prom dress websites on a regular basis. Students sneak over to Newstudyhall.com, a site with more than a hundred mindless games to fritter away time. If iPads are the device of choice in your classroom, you've probably seen the game app *du jour*. (Flappy Bird plagued my room for some time.)

Even when students are on task, there are plenty of inappropriate things they could do to derail a class. At conferences, I'm frequently asked: "How do you manage students? How do you keep them on task and prevent them from doing inappropriate things?"

My answer lacks the silver bullet flash they're probably seeking, but it cuts to the heart of the matter. We can't make students use their time wisely; that decision will always have to be their choice. I'm reminded of the phrase "No Child Left Behind." It's a noble concept, but I've always compared it to a child at a bus stop who refuses to get on the bus. Getting on the bus is his decision; we can only help him make a good decision.

Classroom management in the digital environment mirrors classroom management in the traditional environment. My online spaces—blogs, class website, student-created documents or drawings, or presentations—are treated like the paper and pencil assignments of decades past. If students type something in a backchannel or a blog post, or anything else that's published immediately, it's treated just like they're saying it out loud in front of the class. If they produce work online, it's the same as putting a paper in my old inbox for grading (which I still have buried in a closet somewhere).

Classroom management is classroom management, whether your class is digital or traditional. Nevertheless, I use some maxims to keep my students on task and in bounds. However, rather than a silver bullet, consider them silver BBs: tiny actions that, when used consistently, are effective for shaping classroom behavior.

Circulate frequently. I probably look like I'm walking laps around my classroom. In reality, I'm not trying to burn calories; I'm watching my students as they work. My classroom tables are arranged in a "U" with an inner and an outer U. I'll walk the inner U, then the outer U, then repeat over and over. Being in close proximity lets my students know I'm paying attention. If you prefer to watch from your desk, software exists that enables the teacher's computer to monitor what's going on at student workstations.

Be inquisitive. As I work my way around the classroom, I like to stop, make observations, and ask questions. I'm not giving pop quizzes and hovering to make sure they're being good. (Although, in a roundabout way, I really am!) If someone writes something funny, I'll stop and chuckle. If a student deftly handles a tricky

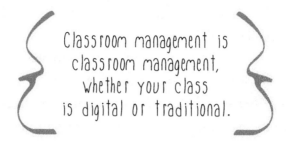

Classroom management is classroom management, whether your class is digital or traditional.

sentence, I'll stop and offer a bit of praise. My goal is to keep observations positive.

Develop relationships and show respect. I teach high school students, and respect is hugely important to them. If they feel as if you're belittling them, some will do everything in their power to make your life miserable. At the beginning of the year, I try to make life easier and happier for everyone by showing them I care about them personally. They know they aren't just another number in my classroom. Laying this foundation early makes a positive difference in day-to-day activities. Jeff Charbonneau, the 2013 National Teacher of the Year, put it best when he said, "I don't have a discipline plan in my classroom. I have a care plan. If you have the latter, you don't need the former."

Set mini-deadlines. When my students work on a long-term project, I often set short-term benchmarks to keep them on task. When my students have several days or longer to work, there's no sense of urgency; they feel no desire to get work accomplished quickly to avoid miscues or delays. It helps to have smaller dead-lines that have a bearing on their final project grade.

Keep it engaging. One truth I learned in college that still applies in this digital age is that nothing helps classroom management like well-written, engaging lesson plans. Creating quality lessons that are relevant and challenging will cure your headaches much better than TYLENOL®.

Sports and prom dress sites will continue to pop up. Even our minds wander during faculty meetings, especially if our laptops are open in front of us. But a little planning and tweaking can decrease those occurrences and increase relevant questions and observations.

‹Chapter 28›
JUMP IN AND TRY

Finally, after compiling them in my mind for months, my plans were finished. My class was going paperless. Totally paperless.

I had twenty-six desktop computers in my classroom. Granted, they were slow-moving, nine-year-old glitchy dinosaurs, but, having taught for so long without any devices in my classroom, I was thankful for them.

For years, I had integrated computer activities into my classwork, but I was ready to take it to the next level. I added bell-ringer activities with online discussion boards, individual student blogs to expand discussions, digital homework activities, and online assessments that were simple to grade and evaluate comprehension. I had an airtight plan… or so I thought.

I laid out my plans to my classes on the first day of school. We jumped right in that week with bell ringers and, *immediately*, the problems hit: log-in issues, slow computer start-up times, blocked websites. Starter activities that usually took only five to ten minutes on paper consumed almost half the class time.

Boom! My paperless class had blown up in my face.

I was bummed out. I had all these big ideas. I believed that less paper and more digital was the right move. In hindsight, it was the right move, but I had gone about it in the wrong way.

Here are a few things I learned from my paperless-class bust that you may want to keep in mind:

1. **Technology for technology's sake isn't good enough.** That old, educational technology maxim was right. Technology has to help the cause. Some of my digital activities actually took longer than using paper and pencil. That's the opposite of what I had intended.

2. **Your hardware must be up to the task.** My bell-ringer activities were good for getting students engaged at the beginning of class, but waiting for slow computers to boot up wasted valuable instructional time. If we had been a one-per-student iPad school, the load time wouldn't have been an issue and students could've been online, working instantly. To have my paperless class, I needed faster technology.

3. **Your tech tools must be up to the task.** I used a documents feature on my learning management system to submit the bell-ringer activities. Unfortunately, while its version of Google Docs was serviceable, there was no way for me to unshare or erase documents shared by students, so the files got collected in my documents folder. I needed a better tool.

4. **Persevere through frustration and failure.** My bust initially made me want to (Gasp!) give up on teaching with technology all together. But I knew I was just jumping to conclusions and refused to give up. I followed through and have since found solutions to many of the problems that slowed us down. Every day, I continue to take strides toward the digital class I envisioned.

Inaction is crippling.
Action is empowering.
Jump in and start.

5. **Take it a step at a time.** In hindsight, it was a mistake to launch all of these paperless initiatives at the same time. I should have phased in the plan little by little. For example, I pushed my students too fast and with too many new tools because I assumed they would pick them up automatically. My students are digital natives, born into this technology-laden culture. They possess a seemingly innate understanding of terms, devices, and processes that many of us, including me, don't have. However, that didn't mean they had an innate ability to instantly learn everything I showed them. I needed to slow down.

After licking my wounds, I moved on and learned from my earlier mistakes. I added new features to my class… but at a slower pace. Bit by bit, my students became more tech-savvy. In the end, we used less paper and incorporated more digital learning tools.

The big lesson I learned from my paperless classroom failure, and from subsequent failures, is to jump in and try! I have become pretty good at gathering new ideas in my head without turning them into reality. You know what happens with those ideas? Nothing. They're trapped in my head. They don't help my students learn, they don't transform learning in my class, and they don't help other educators.

My best ideas can make an impact on my students only when I jump in and try; when my curiosity says, "Hey, that could be really cool in a lesson," and I actually plan an activity and use it. I have to put my fears of failure aside and innovate, even on a small scale. When I step in front of my class and say, "We're going to try something new," and I follow it through to completion—regardless of their initial reactions—that learning transforms into something exciting.

The same is true for you. You've got to jump in and try.

Don't worry that you don't understand every detail about your new idea. Inaction is crippling. Action is empowering. Jump in and start. And if you can't figure something out or your plan busts on Day One, don't worry. Plenty of people, myself included, are ready to help.

⟨Chapter 29⟩
DON'T USE IT ALL

It was a simple job. All I had to do was bury a wire in my backyard. I would grab the shovel, dig a trench, lay the wire in it, and cover it over with dirt.

I told myself it wouldn't take more than an hour. No sweat! Confident in my trench-digging, cable-laying ability, I unraveled all of my wire and put it in place next to the soon-to-be-dug trenches.

Oh, there was one little worrisome factor: only an hour-and-a-half of daylight remained.

The shovel slid into the soil, and I quickly realized digging was more work than I'd expected. "No sweat?" I was soaked before I hit the halfway mark.

The "simple job" ending up taking three times longer than I'd anticipated. And that wire I stretched out so confidently? I forgot and left it in the yard, and my dogs tore it into several pieces!

As you can see, I get excited about things very easily. Sometimes my perception of how things will go is much smoother, faster, and better than reality. Case in point: the beginning of the school year, that glorious time when anything is possible. My students and I start fresh with processes, procedures, and habits.

As the first day of the school year approaches each August, so many new ideas swirl around in my head. I think of how I can streamline my class and incorporate new tools that will spark creativity and take learning to new heights. The more teaching conferences I attend in the summer, the more revolutionary I want my class to be in the fall. I get excited about the possibilities… sometimes a little too excited.

With all this enthusiasm, I spring about thirty-eight new ideas on my poor, unsuspecting students during the first week of school. Perhaps thirty-eight is an exaggeration, but I doubt my kids think so! Their heads spin with my new ideas jumbled in their brains. Even if things go really well, only two or three of the ideas really stick.

My problem? As Queen (the band, not the royal) so eloquently put it, "I want it all… I want it all… I want it all… and I want it NOW!" But I've found that I can't use *all* the new apps and websites I hear about at technology conferences, or *all* the new philosophies I learn in Twitter chats, or *all* the great projects I hear that other teachers are using in their classes.

Why not? Do you remember those students with the spinning heads? Sometimes the amount of head spinning is directly related to the number of new parts I add to class: a new grading policy, or a new website for turning in work, a new language they have to learn in my class, all thrown in with the tech. After adding one too many digital tools to my repertoire, one student told me, "Mr. Miller, we use a *lot* of websites in this class."

Initially, I thought using so many sites was a good thing. My students were experiencing the best of the digital world and were

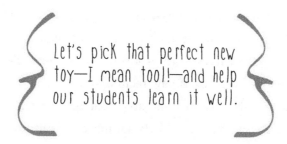

Let's pick that perfect new toy—I mean tool!—and help our students learn it well.

being exposed to tools they could use in other classes and in real life! While there's some truth to that, there's a point of diminishing returns. I'd hit the point where all my additions that were meant to improve class were, instead, making life more complicated. I knew I had to find a happy medium.

Vicki Davis, author of the Cool Cat Teacher blog, shares how she has been intentional about adding new elements to her classes. Rather than trying thirty-eight new things, she adds only one or two major tools to her digital toolbox each year. One year she added wikis, collaborative spaces online where students can edit and add content. Another year she added Evernote, a place to collect, store, and organize ideas. What I love about Vicki's approach is the fact that the new tech is never the focus. What the students are learning and experiencing remains at the forefront. The new tool serves to help students accomplish their educational goals.

We want it all. We want to integrate all the new tools and ideas into our classes, and we want to do it *now*. But we have to be selective and purposeful about the resources we introduce to our students. We don't want them to be like the child on Christmas morning who misses out on some really good toys because she was overloaded with *too many* gifts! Let's pick that perfect new toy—I mean tool!—and help our students learn it well. Help them become masters at wielding that new resource. Help them to know the keyboard shortcuts and extra options that aren't immediately obvious. And help make it stick by showing them how this new tool relates to their lives, both inside and outside the classroom.

Gather new ideas. Find new technology to bring to the classroom. Then, make changes one step at a time. Find a pace that works well for you and your kids. Going overboard or trying to move too fast will only make your students' heads spin.

‹Chapter 30›
MAKE IT

Sal Khan's cousin, Nadia, was struggling in math class. She knew Sal was a smart guy—he had degrees from MIT—so she asked him for help. When he couldn't find any established resources to point her to, Sal created his own.

He started with the Yahoo! Doodle notepad, but found it easier to create and upload videos to YouTube. Sal made more math videos and Nadia kept watching. Over time, her grades, and, more importantly, her comprehension of the subject, improved. Sal discovered, though, that Nadia wasn't the only one watching his videos. As the number of views rose and comments increased, requests for tutoring flooded his inbox. Within a few years, Sal's videos had been watched hundreds of thousands of times!

Today, Sal Kahn is the executive director of Khan Academy, which claims to provide "a free, world-class education for anyone anywhere." Its slate of math videos are now complemented by tutorials on a wide range of subjects, including history, medicine, finance, physics, chemistry, art history, economics, and more.

Millions of students of all ages tap into Khan's resources, which have been translated into dozens of languages.

Here's the lesson for you and me: Khan Academy wouldn't exist if Sal Khan had searched the Internet for math videos, found nothing but junk and said, "I guess I can't help." Instead, because he couldn't find the resource he wanted, *he made it.*

So can you.

Sure, you may find the perfect YouTube video to illustrate a key concept in your class. But chances are it doesn't exist on YouTube or even in commercially produced videos. But if you have a vision of what that perfect video should look like, you probably have the tools surrounding you to create it. The apps and tools available to you online give you the power to create not just the perfect videos, but the perfect book, article, image, and radio show. Below, I've listed a few digital tools that will help you make just about anything you need for your classroom. With these tools and a computer or tablet, you have the ability to craft the perfect learning resource for your students.

A free website creator: Earlier in this book, I explained how a free website became my new digital textbook. Content for my class, student practice activities, and videos for follow-up instruction live on my class website.

A website can be a phenomenal tool for your class. It can be a place to curate great resources to share with students, teachers, or anyone else on the Internet. By enabling discussion tools, like forums or comments, you provide an online space for people to share ideas. If you want to make anything online, a website of your own can give it a home, and it doesn't have to cost you a dime to build it.

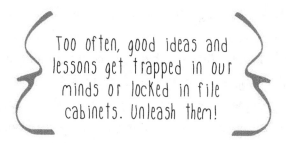

Too often, good ideas and lessons get trapped in our minds or locked in file cabinets. Unleash them!

Videos: The technology in today's smartphones is substantially more powerful than what was used to put a man on the moon. Even a few years ago, the functions these tiny computers offer would have taken tons of expensive technology, including high-definition video cameras and a sophisticated video processing lab. Today, you can pull out your smartphone and, with a few taps on the display, you can record and edit a high-definition video. You can even add music, annotations, and other features using video editor apps. Then, publish it on YouTube, and your video can be viewed on the second-largest search engine in the world! With billions of searches each month, YouTube allows you to share your videos with the world. Or you can choose to keep your videos private; the choice is yours.

Flashcard Websites: Flashcards don't sit very high up on Bloom's taxonomy for higher-order thinking, but they're a great resource for classes that require memorization. In fact, many of my students like using online flashcards in my class so much they've started creating them for their other subjects! Students or teachers can create flashcard sets through sites such as Quizlet, ExamTime and StudyBlue. Once created, the cards are accessible via a link provided by the site. Since many flashcard sites have mobile apps, students can keep vocabulary or key concepts in their pockets and practice anywhere.

Google Apps: Making documents, presentations, spreadsheets, and drawings accessible to others is easy with Google Apps. When shared, these files can be accessed with a link or through other users' Google accounts. Online materials can then be edited by multiple people in real time, which means changes are instantly visible. I often create new content for my classes using Google Docs and then share the links on my class website.

We live in a consumption-heavy, digital society. Most people go online in search of something: a website, song, video, or worksheet. While the vast majority of Internet users consume information, only a small percentage creates it. Smaller still is the percentage that creates *and shares*. We've already discussed the importance of sharing, but I want to stress this point: As teachers, we succeed by learning from others. Think of all of the people who have helped you become the educator you are today. It may have been the teacher across the hall who served as a sounding board or a shoulder to cry on. Maybe it was a colleague who shared great ideas, or even someone you'll never meet in a country you'll never visit who posted a resource online.

Now, think of the impact you could have on other educators who could benefit from all you've learned and experienced. Too often, good ideas and lessons get trapped in our minds or locked in file cabinets. Unleash them! Turn your ideas into resources, and then put them where they can help others. Go make something!

‹Chapter 31›
Stay In Touch with Students

A couple of years ago I got Minecraft blocked at my school. Now, I wish I hadn't. Minecraft is a sandbox-style game in which players can customize a virtual world. They can build or destroy, dig caverns, or create tall monuments. They can create for the sake of creating or, with the game in "survival mode," build a world that must sustain them.

One day, I found a few students making worlds on the computers in my homeroom class. One had made an elaborate building that had taken hours and, instead of trying to hide it from me, he was proud of his work and wanted to share it with me. I was amazed and impressed. Students were creating, learning, and developing their creativity, all on their own time.

So what did I do? Being a new teacher at my school who wanted to do the "right" thing, I informed the technology director. It was one of those "I didn't know if you knew, but…" types of emails. Minecraft was blocked within the next few days. My frustrated students were forced to abandon their virtual construction efforts… at least at school.

Dumb, dumb, dumb.

I view Minecraft in a totally different light now. Today there's an entire movement to use Minecraft in education. Elementary school teachers have used it to teach math concepts and digital literacy, as well for a lunchtime activity. I *wish* I had thought outside the box earlier and realized the game's true potential. Instead, I overlooked a crucial component of keeping education relevant and missed a golden opportunity to stay in touch with my students.

I've since installed Minecraft on my own iPad so my children—ages five, seven, and nine—can play it. It's been fun to watch them learn the game and pick up lessons they don't get in a traditional classroom. For example, they've learned:

- It's possible to dig a hole or tunnel so deep that there's no easy way to get yourself out. (I think there's an important figurative lesson there.)

- Unexpected things can be useful. They have recently learned fire and lava melt ice, and now they're creating using these new tools. For instance, my daughter built a volcano and filled it with lava.

- How to plan ahead and reap the reward. By adding animals to their worlds, they learned that sheep can be sheared and their wool harvested for use or trade.

They're playing, but they're also creating and learning. They're experimenting with trial and error, a skill they'll need in the world they'll be growing into.

Teachers who pay attention to students' lives and interests and incorporate them into their class give students the opportunity to see themselves in the curriculum. When they see themselves, they see the relevance. Geometry doesn't hold any relevance to a student until he realizes how crucial it is to constructing a building or hitting a great shot in pool.

If you follow fantasy football, you're probably familiar with Matthew Berry, an ESPN columnist and fantasy football pundit. Unlike most fantasy football pieces, his widely read columns don't focus on nuts-and-bolts facts or predictions. Instead, Berry taps into popular culture and his own life... sometimes just to tell a story and sometimes to illustrate a point about football. When he started working at ESPN, the company asked him to which magazines he wanted subscriptions so he could keep on the cutting edge of his profession. The magazine that topped his list? *People.* Why *People* and not *Sports Illustrated?* Because *People* helped him connect with his readers in ways that his fantasy football colleagues missed. The result? Berry's columns stood out from the rest and he developed a huge following.

As teachers, we can do the same thing. Want to stay relevant with students? Learn about what they like. Listen to their music. Read the websites they frequent. Observe. Listen to what they talk about. Ask lots of questions about their interests and lives. Even if the answers don't show up in your classes, the relationships you'll develop will yield great returns.

And, if your students share their awesome digital Minecraft creations with you, think twice about tattling on them to the technology director. You might regret it!

ON THE BLOG:
MORE RESOURCES FOR USING MINECRAFT IN THE CLASSROOM

<Chapter 32>
MAKE IT VISUAL

In my classroom, I'm known as the "King of the Stick Figure." If we're creating a story in my Spanish class or practicing vocabulary terms, my stick figures, complete with shoes, hair, a cane, a top hat, etc., inhabit the board. (As soon as I branch out beyond stick figures, I lose my crown and my king status!)

It turns out my doodling habit, which creates what could loosely be called art, is a better idea than I had ever imagined. In an earlier chapter, I mentioned the picture superiority effect,[1] the belief that even poor quality images—including my stick figures—have a much greater impact on learning than the best text-based presentation.

Brain research shows us that combining pictures and words is effective because of the dual-coding theory that suggests that our memories are stored verbally, visually, or both. Words are encoded in the brain verbally and are remembered only as words. Images, however, are encoded verbally and visually and are remembered as words and pictures. This dual coding gives images an advantage.

Consider all of the educational resources that work directly *against* this idea. PowerPoint presentations are the most obvious example. Too often these text-heavy slides reveal a love of bulleted lists and the bad habit of writing down every word we want to say. In reality, our attempts to make an impact have likely yielded the opposite result. If we want to inspire, a bulleted list isn't going to do it. We'd be far better off writing less, using fewer words, and adding illustrations.

The two most common excuses about using pictures in the classroom are ones I've used personally. Raise your hand if you've ever said (or thought) either one of these concerns:

I'm not an artist, so this won't work for me. Honestly, I'm not much of an artist. I rely heavily on stick figures and even have to explain some of my drawings to my students. But that's the beauty of doodling! If you draw a blob and tell your audience it's a cloud, they'll imagine it as a cloud. Even better, you can draw the same blob and call it a bush or thought bubble, and your audience will follow right along in their imagination. So, you don't have to be an artist. Just keep it simple.

If you don't want to create your own custom drawing, that's fine, too. Choose from the terabytes of images available to you online. Chances are you can find a picture that will work if you take a little time to "go fishing" for the right one.

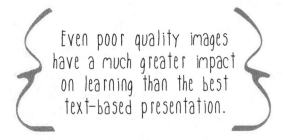

Even poor quality images have a much greater impact on learning than the best text-based presentation.

Using pictures isn't legitimate academic work. In the past, I believed writing and reading were the "hallmarks" of great education, and should be the focus in the classroom. But why do we read? To get ideas into our brains, right? Literacy is of great importance in every class, but if our brains try to eventually encode ideas as pictures anyway, why not speed the process with pictures? Some students struggle to make a mental picture of what we're talking about. If we can help them do what their brain is already trying to do, we have a better chance of helping kids learn and remember the material.

So, how do we create these pictures? There are lots of options:

- **Creative Commons Image Searches.** A huge trove of pictures licensed for reuse is available to anyone. Go to search.creativecommons.org to check them out. While you can use these images without worrying about violating copyright law, remember to attribute your source when you use them.

- **Drawing Apps.** Paper app for the iPad by FiftyThree makes what I create much prettier than anything I could draw on regular paper. The app and everything in it is free and you can save your work as an image file for use in other places.

- **Learn How to Draw.** *The Sketchnote Handbook* by Mike Rohde offers practical tips on how to easily turn your ideas into images. What I learned from Rohde is that practically anything you want to draw can be made from basic shapes, lines, and dots. For example, he suggests drawing people using a rectangle for their bodies, lines for arms and legs, and a circle for their heads. From there it's easy to make them fancier with clothes and accessories.

Getting visual isn't only about pictures. Video often equals instant engagement in my classroom. Students like to record videos—especially when they get to use their phones—but they like to watch them even more. And if those videos are produced by their peers, their interest skyrockets generating power that has huge potential to be harnessed for educational gain.

Video creation tools abound and more hit the market every day. Windows Movie Maker (Windows) and iMovie (iOS) come bundled with many new computers. WeVideo is a great web-based video editing tool, and its free version accommodates the needs of most classrooms. Integrating video projects into the classroom can be as simple or complex as you want. Just grab a phone, digital camera or tablet, and your students are on their way.

The key is to give these visual ideas a shot. Incorporate sketching into your lessons, whether on the whiteboard or on an iPad app. Stimulate your students' thinking by choosing from the millions of photos available online. Create videos, or turn your students loose as videographers. Use pictures to support your lessons and see the difference it makes in your class.

ON THE BLOG:
THE REASON I'M RETHINKING
MY DIGITAL CLASSROOM

10 Video Ideas For (Almost) Any Classroom

1. **Create a personal narrative:** Students can create a narrative about themselves, a character, or a historical person. Record video clips from many different facets of the subject's life. Add a voiceover to tell the story and music to set the mood.

2. **Tell a story:** Stories intrigue us. They draw us in and take us to a place and time we've never been. Using concepts from class and connecting them to stories could have a huge impact on student learning.

3. **Create a whiteboard animation:** Set up a recording device (smartphone, tablet, or video camera) on a tripod so it won't move and aim it at a whiteboard or chalkboard. Push RECORD and start drawing. Use video editing tools to speed up the recording to four times its normal speed and add a voiceover and music.[2]

4. **Record a screencast demonstration:** Beneficial to teachers and students, free screencasting sites like Screencast-O-Matic and Screenr turn student computers into simple video creation tools. Students can show a slide presentation with audio descriptions or demonstrate how to do something on their computers. Teachers can easily flip instruction in this way.

5. **Give a video message with a speaking avatar:** Avatars aren't recorded with cameras, but they are video and can be created quickly and easily. Free sites like Voki allow users to create "talking heads" with custom messages. You can create avatars of some historical characters and speak for them. Students can create these videos in response to something learned. You can also use Vokis to communicate substitute teacher lesson plans.

6. **Make a tour of a significant location:** Anytime students visit a place, on a field trip or on vacation, for example, they can share their learning experience with others by recording video and narrating it as they go. If they can't visit a place personally, creating a video slide show with Animoto or in a screencast works, too. Take it to the next level by screencasting a trip through a city or important landmarks using Google Earth!

7. **Create Vines of vocabulary terms:** Vine is the social media site that allows users to create and share six-second looping video clips. Students can use iOS, Android, and Windows devices to create Vines. If Vine is not allowed in your school district, the videos can be downloaded for offline access. One way students could use Vines is to show a vocabulary word on paper and then show a visual representation of the term. Post these on a class Weebly site and vocabulary learning is redefined!

8. **Create GIF examples of classroom content:** GIFs are moving image files, silent video that's treated like a picture file. By using a free GIF maker,[3] students can create videos of anything class-related and post it on a class website.

9. **Highlight a cause:** When students take action to address a community or global issue, the result is more than learning. It's change for the better. Students can contribute to something bigger than themselves by using their video skills to encourage others to take action as well.

10. **Dream:** Put a "What if?" spin on classroom learning and your activity immediately moves to synthesis, the second-highest level of Bloom's taxonomy. Challenge students to speculate what would happen if something in history happened differently or if a character in a story made a different decision. Video is a great medium to play out those ideas.

10 Video Ideas for
Specific Subject Areas

1. Recreate a historic speech or moment in history for a social studies class.

2. Display the work and results of a science lab project from hypothesis to conclusion. Add images of lab data in the project to show specifics of the results.

3. Write and record poetry or short stories illustrating literary elements learned in an English class. Include Creative Commons or public domain music that matches the mood of the written work.

4. Bring story problems to life or record a whiteboard explanation of a math problem. Use subtitles to further explain concepts in the problem.

5. Create a conversation, explanation, or skit in another language for a foreign language class.

6. Show off skills learned in a physical education lesson or impart wisdom for a healthy lifestyle for a health class.

7. Give cooking demonstrations or child development presentations for family and consumer-science classes.

8. Record video presentations to take agriculture classes outside the school's walls, giving demonstrations of live animals, crops, or anything Ag-related.

9. Highlight service projects or school spirit events hosted by extra-curricular groups.

10. Send parent and student reminders from the guidance office and make connections from the principal's office in regular video messages.

<Chapter 33>
GO WHERE THE KIDS ARE

I'm frequently impressed by my students' tech savvy.
They manage accounts on multiple social media sites. They have mastered the nuances of writing messages online to convey their ideas. They curate apps tailored to their needs, share the best with friends, and can provide detailed explanations of why the worst don't work. If I need to talk through the pros and cons of the latest iOS update or a new app I'm considering, my students are usually the best conversationalists.

Theirs is a digital world.

In contrast, their classrooms, by and large, are lacking in technology and littered with textbooks. (You already know how I feel about those!) Students listen to lectures when they'd rather find answers faster through Google searches, Twitter questions, and YouTube videos. They write in workbooks, complete worksheets, and carry heavy paper notebooks, but they'd prefer to use digital devices to keep track of everything they need to remember and all they've created. Students live in a digital world, but we force them to learn through analog means. No wonder keeping them interested is so tough!

We have a choice to make: We can move into the house next door to our students' digital homes, and embrace social media, digital tools, and online research, or we can force them to take the bus to the Town of Academia, home of traditional teaching methods and tools that no longer relate to their lives. It's a complex issue, but I know what I'm going to do; I'm moving in next door as quickly as possible.

In my opinion, the changing marketplace and continually advancing technology require us to reevaluate the way we educate. Tapping into technology is crucial to getting buy-in from our students and truly engaging them in the learning process. A constant bombardment from today's continually updating, on-demand society screams for their attention. Schools have tried blocking sites (I still can't believe I got Minecraft banned!), limiting Internet access, and prohibiting phone use in schools. But what if we took a different approach, one that serves our purposes as educators *and* supports our students' desire to learn and use technology? Rather than fight the current, let's use it to our advantage.

Throughout this book, I've shared a variety of tech tools and strategies that have helped me break through the noise. My goal is to use the tools and platforms with which kids *enjoy* engaging to teach them how to learn, communicate, and thrive in today's world. Now, I'd like to share one of my favorite examples of how technology and social media have worked to support learning in my classroom.

Social media is viewed by many teachers as a time-waster. And sure, it can be. But it's also a great place to connect with peers, learn about leaders, and get up-to-the-second news. Twitter, a social media platform with 288 million monthly active users[1], is a go-to place for my students. It's where they express their opinions and keep up with what's happening in the world. They share

> Students live in a
> digital world,
> but we force them to
> learn through analog means.

pieces of their lives through words, hashtags, and pictures, one-hundred-forty characters at a time.

So where do Twitter and school connect? Really, it can be anything fun, interesting, or even just daily life. One particularly memorable shared moment came during my school's homecoming week. Throughout the week, everyone dresses up for spirit days before the big football game. Each day has a different theme. Since so many of my school's students love to hunt, the *"Duck Dynasty* Day,"* was a huge hit. (If you aren't familiar with *Duck Dynasty*, it's an A&E reality show about the Robertson family's duck call business and the fun and hijinks of clean, country living.) The students really went over the top. They dressed up in camouflage, wore their *Duck Dynasty* T-shirts, and sported long beards. One student even brought his official Si Robertson iced tea glass and pitcher.

Because we happened to be studying family relationship vocabulary in Spanish 1 that week, it made sense to chart out the Robertson family tree, labeling the relationships in Spanish. We used AETV.com to find the family tree... even though most of my students already knew all the Robertson family members' names and relationships by heart.

Cool activity on a fun day, right? But that was just the beginning.

When we finished, I said, "We should post this on Twitter and tag some of the *Duck Dynasty* guys. Maybe they'll retweet it."

(Retweeting is when someone sees your Twitter post and shares, or *retweets*, it to his or her followers.)

The kids agreed. Using my iPad and several students' phones, we took pictures of them standing next to the chart and then tweeted the pictures using our personal Twitter accounts. We tagged a couple of people from the show using their Twitter names. We knew that we had a better chance of getting retweeted if our Twitter blitz caught their attention.

I started by sending a tweet to Duck Dynasty CEO, Willie Robertson, and his brother Jase Robertson. Within five minutes, Jase saw the tweet and thought it was cool enough to retweet to his *1.2 million Twitter followers*. The kids went nuts over their day of Twitter fame. Jase Robertson, a guy they watched and loved from *Duck Dynasty*, had seen and liked their picture and shared it with his fans!

Word spread quickly, as it tends to do in high school hallways. The kids shared it on their own Twitter accounts, and the school's Facebook page posted the picture and the story to families and the community. It even made the local newspaper. Within two days, the tweet had 128 retweets and 181 "favorites."

Maybe you're thinking, *Great, a celebrity retweeted a picture of your students. What exactly, does that have to do with education?* Well, a lot. For one, it affirmed their Spanish studies. They worked in class to learn some new vocabulary; if they hadn't, none of this would have happened. It also proved that good things happen when you give something your all, like these students did by getting decked out in *Duck Dynasty* garb. Social media, specifically Twitter, along with *Duck Dynasty*, AETV.com, and a digital picture helped them connect their efforts to something they love. And I'll bet they'll never forget that Jase, one of the Robertson *hermanos* liked their picture. They needed to learn the vocabulary. I could have just handed them a worksheet and textbook. Instead, they got excited about the day's lesson because technology made it real to them.

****

A colleague once challenged my ideas of ditching textbooks, arguing that students will be required to use textbooks, listen to lectures, and write papers in college. Some professors certainly lean heavily on texts and lectures, but college isn't the end game: knowing how to learn in today's society is. Plus, colleges are integrating more technology as well as advanced teaching and learning techniques every day.

Momentum is building toward twenty-first century learning. We must prepare students for the world they're going to live in— not the one we grew up in. Let's equip them to learn in a way that's parallel to how their brain is wired. For example, outside the classroom they don't write by hand; they type. They don't passively receive information; they search for it, interact with it, and share it. We have to be willing to revolutionize our approach to teaching if we're going empower students to succeed. If living in their world equips me to capture their attention and focus it on my message, I'll do it.

ON THE BLOG:
THE PASSION THAT DRIVES
ME AS A TEACHER

SECTION 4

DITCH THAT CURRICULUM

Ditching your textbooks and their pre-planned curriculum can feel liberating. Imagine having complete freedom—within the context of your district's guidelines, of course—to decide what to teach and how to teach it. *Ahhhh.*

But a split second after you make the ditching decision, the reality of what it means to be in complete control of your classroom's curriculum dawns on you. Fear strikes at your elation and panic works to put you back on the boring, textbook-marked path.

Take a breath. You can do this. In the final few chapters, we'll walk through a plan for establishing your teaching philosophy and developing a curriculum that works for you and your students, and meets all your school's requirements.

Yes, you can do this. And my bet is that once you ditch your textbooks, you'll never go back to them.

‹Chapter 34›
Establish Your Philosophy

During the first month of my rookie teaching year I agreed to help with the Fellowship of Christian Athletes (FCA) club. In our small school, the FCA membership filled only three rows of the high school's 1,000-seat auditorium. As a warm-up activity at the first meeting, we played a trivia game. The FCA student leader gave the students a task I was sure my Spanish-class students would dominate: "Say something in another language."

Excitedly, I looked over to a group my students with half a smirk on my face and said, "All of you should be able to do this!"

I was the Spanish teacher. They were Spanish students. Granted, I'd only had them in class for a couple of weeks, but certainly they could say something, right?

One hand went up. One.

When the leader called on this lone brave girl, she spouted off a sentence—in *Hungarian*—that she'd learned on a mission trip to Hungary.

The rest of the auditorium? Crickets. No hands up. No Spanish. The silence crushed my first-year, Spanish teacher soul.

In that moment, I decided what I wanted to be known for: teaching students to *speak* Spanish. I wanted my *students* to be known for their ability to *speak* the language. They didn't have to be fluent, and their grammar didn't have to be perfect. But I wanted them to be able to carry on a simple conversation if they ever traveled to Mexico or met someone who spoke Spanish.

The motivation to ditch that textbook isn't only—or even mostly—driven by a desire to go paperless or create technology-powered lessons; it's about *purpose*. What do you want to do with the powerful platform you've been given?

As a teacher, you have an enormous influence on your students. It would be a shame to miss a valuable opportunity because you didn't have a clear purpose and a plan to fulfill it. As Benjamin Franklin famously said, "He who fails to plan is planning to fail." Reverse curriculum planning will help establish your teaching philosophy so you can create an effective plan. Start with the end goal in mind, then work your way backward. To find your starting point, answer the following questions:

- What kind of teacher are you?

- What do you want to be known for?

- What do you want your students to be known for?

- What do you want your students to be able to do at the end of the year?

- What skills do they need to develop for success?

- What discussions do they need to have to cultivate new ideas?

Look inside first. Define who you are and how you want to be known as a teacher. Then look outside yourself for the tools and support to create a plan and put it in motion. Connecting with other educators on Twitter, reading good books, and following blogs can spark ideas and enthusiasm. The new ideas you encounter may help you transform your teaching, but they may also challenge your beliefs. That's okay. We don't progress without challenge.

For example, the first time I visited the standards-based learning Twitter chat (#sblchat), I read numerous stances on educational philosophy that ran counter to mine. My first instinct was to fight back; my next was to give up and move on. But I stayed, swallowed my pride, listened, and asked questions. I've since changed my stance on homework and redoing work, and I believe I'm a better teacher as a result.

Who do you want to be as a teacher? Who do you want your students to be? Whether you make a conscious decision about it or not, you're making a decision. The words you say in class, the activities you include, and the way you carry yourself are all manifestations of your teaching philosophy. You can intentionally make those parts of yourself and your class what you want them to be, or you can hope they fall perfectly into place.

Hope isn't a viable teaching strategy. Don't fail to plan. Define your purpose. Craft your philosophy, test it against what respected peers are doing, and then put together a plan to help your students succeed. Your legacy is too important to leave to chance.

On the Blog:
10 Ways Google's Philosophy can Guide Teachers

‹Chapter 35›
CREATE A MISSION STATEMENT

Teachers are like pilots. They journey with their passengers (students) from a starting place to a fixed destination. They set waypoints that must be crossed to arrive safely on schedule. Like pilots, teachers chart the appropriate course based on experience and knowledge. The work students produce provides feedback like the warning lights and gauges of a plane.

Before a pilot taxies a plane to the runway, he must know his destination. Teachers are no different. They need to know what they're going to teach and who they want to be. Your professional mission statement identifies your destination: your end goal. It doesn't have to be etched on a plaque hanging in your classroom, but it's helpful to clearly identify your mission as a teacher.

Jessica Balsley, author of The Art of Education blog, suggests these tips for writing a professional mission statement:

- Keep it under thirty words.
- Incorporate characteristics about yourself and how you interact with others.
- Think about: "My perfect world is a place where…"

My professional mission statement? I want my students to converse easily in Spanish. Sure, I want them to develop vocabulary and grammar skills, and grow in cultural understanding, but fluid conversational Spanish is the stamp I want to put on my teaching. When my students leave my classroom for the last time, I don't want them to freeze if someone walks up to them and says, "*¿Cómo estás?*" or "*¿Dónde está la oficina?*" My mission guides everything I do as a Spanish teacher, from crafting units that promote great opportunities to converse in Spanish to planning lessons that hone my students' speaking and listening skills.

If writing a traditional mission statement doesn't interest you, put an educational twist on the book *One Word That Will Change Your Life* by Dan Britton, Jimmy Page, and Jon Gordon. Pick one word to describe what you want in an entire school year. Instead of setting resolutions like we often do on New Year's Day—fifty percent of which are forgotten within a month—the authors suggest selecting a single word to embody the theme of an entire year.

The authors, who are leaders in the Fellowship of Christian Athletes organization, outline a process for selecting "the word" for a year:

1. **Look in.** Get somewhere quiet where you can focus and ask yourself three questions: What do I need? What's in my way? What needs to go?

2. **Look up.** As Christians, they suggest connecting with God, who reveals your word to you through prayer and quiet reflection.

3. **Live your word.** Designate three ways to make sure you have regular reminders of your word. Share your word with three people who are close to you, and make yourself accountable to them.

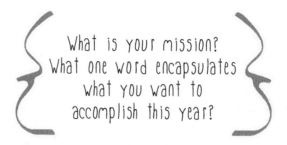

What is your mission?
What one word encapsulates
what you want to
accomplish this year?

Selecting a precise word to describe the change you want to make in various areas of your teaching life—or your life in general—can be simple and powerful. Your word can become the lens through which you view your interaction with students and the filter you use to decide how you will plan and deliver your lessons.

One year, I chose the word "create," in part because of the following statistics I heard on a Google Educast podcast:

- One percent of students are creators,
- Nine percent of students are curators, and
- Ninety percent are consumers of digital content.

My goal was to boost the creation factor. I wanted my students to create products that mattered and to share them with their classmates, their school, and the world. I also wanted to create more as a teacher so I could share more with my students, parents, and peers. Focused on my word, I led my students to create RSA-style whiteboard animations and write Choose-Your-Own-Adventure stories using Google Forms. That one word—*create*—drove everything I did that year. It was my destination, the blinking beacon in the distance.

What is your mission? What one word encapsulates what you want to accomplish this year? In the next chapter, we'll discuss creating a plan for getting to your destination, but first, you must decide where you want to go.

Chapter 36

IDENTIFY MAJOR THEMES

Your destination—your mission statement—is charted. Now it's time to start some big-picture curriculum planning.

Ditching your textbooks frees you to teach your own way. You don't have to follow someone else's pre-set, outdated, or uninteresting plan. But you *do* need a plan. In keeping with the teacher/pilot metaphor, a curriculum plan is like a flight plan. Pilots need to know their destination, but they also have to create and submit a flight plan before they can take off. And the course charted is rarely a straight line. To avoid storms or restricted airspaces, pilots set waypoints that lead them on a safe path around those obstacles. As a teacher, your waypoints are the major themes that comprise the entire year's curriculum.

What major themes will help you reach your final destination and fulfill your mission? You may have the freedom to determine some of your waypoints; others may be predetermined by national or state content standards or by district or school policy. Gather your must-haves so you can appropriately distribute them throughout your curriculum.

Here's how curriculum planning plays out in my Spanish classes. My major themes consist of eight thematic units. Some examples include haves, needs, wants, vacations, and being a student (all in Spanish 1), and environment, health, and education (in Advanced Placement Spanish). All of the vocabulary, grammar, and culture topics I want to cover can be grouped into these themes. The themes also provide conversation starters for classroom discussions. Even Spanish 1 students can describe their favorite vacation getaways and the joys and perils of student life because they're included within these themes.

Without this type of big-picture planning, it's easy to get focused on the nuts and bolts of the content and miss out on gems of teaching, such as meaningful discussions, that should be part of education. I regularly have to silence my inner grammarian and get back to true conversation—sloppy sentences and all, because conversation is at the core of what I teach my students.

Once your waypoints—or major themes—are planned, it's time to create your pre-flight checklist. Before a massive jet carrying hundreds of passengers heads to the runway, its pilot and flight crew run through a checklist to confirm everything is functioning properly.

Landing gear? Check.

Wing flaps? Check.

Hydraulic systems? Check.

As teachers, our pre-flight checklists consist of the skills we want our students to develop, the information and processes we want them to learn, and the experiences we want them to have. In the past, textbooks determined what was most important, but, if we're ditching our textbooks, we can now arrange, modify, take away from, and add items as we see fit.

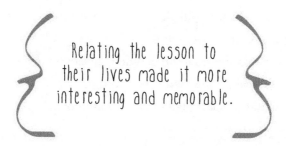

Relating the lesson to their lives made it more interesting and memorable.

Multiple checklists are necessary to ensure a class becomes the learning experience we want it to be. Your first checklist identifies any applicable academic standards, policies, or requirements determined by your state, Common Core, district, or corporation. These are the immutable laws of our classroom and should be a high priority. Beyond the requirements, create a second checklist using your major curriculum themes. As you consider each of your themes, determine the skills to master, content to cover, and experiences to soak in. A third checklist could include essential questions that should be answered or addressed during instruction.

When I ditched my textbooks, I restructured my classes around major themes and created pre-flight checklists to measure my students' progress. Using a copy of my state world language standards and my major themes, I listed the critical skills students needed. During this process, I discovered that some of my themes needed modification. For example, I had always taught the verb *querer* (to want) in a lesson about *e* to *ie* stem-changing verbs. But my Spanish 1 theme of *haves, wants, and needs*, required this verb to be taught earlier in the year. I had never broken up the content that way before, but it made sense and strengthened the theme-based unit.

For each of my theme-based units, I developed a couple of essential questions that cut to the core of the topic. I then addressed those questions throughout the unit. For example, in the *why I am how I am* theme, we addressed the following questions:

- What was my family like when I was young?
- What was I like when I was young?
- How did others make me who I am now?

The questions weren't exceptionally introspective, but they allowed for some interesting, thought-provoking conversations... in Spanish, no less. As we checked off the target grammatical concepts of using a past tense, we also discussed differences and similarities of the students and their families, as well as their hopes for the future. Relating the lesson to their lives made it more interesting and memorable.

When your major themes and checklists are in place, you can then create a consistent structure to follow as you plan. For each of my classes I created a four-page plan for the year. Each page represented one of the four grading periods of the year and contained a section for every week of the grading period. For every section, I listed:

- holidays, important school dates, and any conflicts that might affect instruction;
- the theme covered in the unit;
- activities, projects, and discussions;
- academic standards and policies incorporated; and
- any assessments (formative or summative).

This simple structure is a convenient reference for creating daily lesson plans. Start with the big picture, and then narrow your focus by determining your waypoints. Whether you want to create daily plans for the entire year or a week or two at a time, be sure to allow for modification of plans based on changing pace, remediation, and other factors.

<Chapter 37>

BE READY TO ADJUST

My personal situation was ideal for ditching my textbooks. High school Spanish has no prerequisite classes. And, in my small school district, I teach all levels of Spanish. Major changes to my curriculum don't affect other teachers or courses that my students will take.

Ditching textbooks is certainly easier for teachers whose courses don't depend on what students learned in past classes or on what they need to know for the next teacher's class. Similarly, it's easier to teach your own way when you don't have colleagues teaching the same classes. However, if you're in a school with multiple teachers in your content area, or if you teach classes with higher or lower levels that you don't teach, you can still ditch your textbooks; you'll just need to make some adjustments. You may, for example, need to limit the range of content to be covered in your class so as not to overlap the prescribed curriculum of teachers who are using textbooks as a guide. In fact, if you're in this situation, you can review and use others' textbooks as guides— modifying, removing, adding, and adjusting the content and flow to fit your class goals.

Teaching a class using the *Ditch That Textbook* method frees teachers and students to enjoy opportunities for creativity, which might not have existed when teaching chapter-by-chapter from the textbook. In the end, I'm confident that if even one teacher in a school is brave enough to ditch his or her textbooks, everyone in the school will benefit from this relevant, engaging, and exciting approach to learning.

That being said, revolutionaries always encounter challenges. If you set out to ditch your textbooks—or any textbook mentalities—expect there to be days when things blow up in your face. Know now that there will be times when a technology component won't work with your school's Internet filter, or a lesson's message fails to resonate with students. That's okay. Dave Burgess, social studies teacher and author of *Teach Like a PIRATE*, tells a story about what he thought was going to be an awesome lesson on Orson Wells's *War of the Worlds*. He had created an old-fashioned radio as a prop for the lesson and had students listen to it in the dark for extra effect. But the lesson went awry. Students horsed around in the dark and didn't pay attention. At first, his students' behavior frustrated Dave. Upon reflection, he realized something: it's no wonder the kids weren't interested. In today's world, old-fashioned radio broadcasts are boring! Instead of scrapping his idea and never returning to it again, he learned from his experiences and revamped the lesson to make it more effective.

When lessons go wrong, roll with the punches. Be flexible. Don't be too hard on yourself. Learn from your mistakes, and improve your approach for the next time. Your students will forgive you when they see that you're willing to try new things and make school more relevant to them.

<Chapter 38>

TAKE YOUR TIME

It takes time to create a textbook-less environment. In the end, it doesn't pay to rush. Take your time. When you create a new unit, give yourself time to think about how you really want it to look.

I once heard a keynote speaker suggest that teachers create new multi-week units one year at a time. That didn't sound fast enough to me, so I jumped into the process with both feet, revamping my curriculum for three levels in a matter of months. I made unit plans, created essential questions, and even did some basic lesson planning. I regret going so fast. When I looked over the planning done in such a hurry, all of the lessons looked the same. Rather than creating multiple, unique units, I had essentially copied and pasted the same unit and made some adjustments. Nevertheless, I still take exception to the speaker's advice. I don't like the idea of doing one new unit a year. With four levels of Spanish and six to eight units in each one, it would take me twenty-four to thirty-two years to create the curriculum I envision! (For the record, I don't plan to still be teaching high school Spanish thirty-two years

> Pick one or two new tools
> or strategies that will help
> you achieve *your* objectives
> for the next grading period.

from now. I envision playing more golf and enjoying time with my grandchildren.)

What's the solution? Create new units thoughtfully and consider them individually.

Based on the nature of the content and your level of comfort with different units, some are going to be easier to plan than others. Momentum is a powerful force. As such, when planning, start with the units with which you're most comfortable, those that will be easiest to complete. There's magic to checking those items off your list; you'll be encouraged to keep going when you see that you're making progress toward your goal.

There is, however, some bad news to all this creating and rearranging. Change is slow, and difficult, and messy. Change is hard, especially when the entire system is set up against you. Education has been virtually the same for more than a century. Like a boulder rolling down a mountain, propelled by momentum, outdated education practices are tough to stop or even shift in direction—especially if you try to do it alone.

I faced this boulder when I made a few big changes in my classroom at once. The two biggest changes were going (mostly) paperless in favor of Google Apps for Education and connecting my classes to others by way of Skype. For the most part, both transitions happened successfully. My class created and collaborated with Google Apps in ways that they hadn't before. My students met and spoke Spanish with classes from the United States and Spain, and we set up second and third Skypes to continue the collaborative learning experience.

Still, many days in my class feel the same as they have for years. Those frustrating days make me wonder, "Am I really the solution to the irrelevant school's problem, or am I contributing to it?"

And then I step back for perspective. I remind myself that my dedication to create an atmosphere that will better prepare my students for their uncertain future takes daily effort. I recommit to taking one step at a time, persisting over the weeks, months, and years.

Maintaining the patience required for long-term change can be hard for me, especially when I see daily posts and videos about great educators and the exceptional things they're doing. Being the self-reflective person I am, I often have the same reaction: "Wow, that's great! Look at what that teacher is doing. Look what her students have created. Look at the impact her classroom is having on the world."

And I wonder, "Why am I not doing that? Why aren't my students doing that? What kind of a teacher am I if we're not doing that? I hope I'm not doing them a disservice."

Sometimes, the reaction is more like this: "I'd really like to try this new tool and integrate it in my class. Wow, it's kind of complicated. But these other teachers are embracing it, and their students are succeeding. I hope I'm not doing my students a disservice."

Who knew teaching would be such a vicious roller coaster of emotion?! I'm guessing I'm not the only one who has experienced this kind of let down. I've come to an important conclusion: I just can't do it all. I can do only what I can do. And that's okay. Another teacher is going to use different teaching techniques than I do and have great success. That's okay. There will be lots of sites and apps and ideas worth using, and there will be many of them that I can't or won't get to. That's okay, too. As much as I'd like to jump in and start all of my new ideas all at once, I know that doing so is a recipe for disaster. Remember my first attempt at a paperless classroom?

I just can't do it all. Neither can you. And that's okay. Review *your* mission statement, *your* major themes, *your* checklists, and then pick one or two new tools or strategies that will help you achieve *your* objectives for the next grading period. Then, give yourself and your students the necessary time to learn the new process or master the new technology. Take your time. When you have that down, add the next tool or strategy to your repertoire. Create the class you want by committing to take one step at a time, and persisting over the weeks, months, and years.

Conclusion

We've just spent more than 40,000 words together. We have considered why heading toward the digital realm is the way to go. We have covered several mindsets that can either steer you toward unhappiness and frustration or toward fulfillment and rejuvenation. We've gone over some techniques and ideas for ditching your textbooks, and we've outlined how you can ditch your curriculum, too.

So, where do we go now? It's time for some action. But that doesn't mean I'm going to put some blank lines on the following pages and force you to write ideas on them. If you're like me, those lines in books just stay blank. *Action* means taking that proverbial first step in the journey of many miles. Here are some ways to get started:

Have a conversation. This could be the most personal and powerful way of working through any changes you're considering. Sit down over a cup of coffee with a colleague. Send an e-mail to someone whose opinion you respect. Send me a tweet including my Twitter username, @jmattmiller, and the hashtag #DitchBook, to join conversations about the book. If I don't have an answer, I'll pass it along to smart people who probably will!

A conversation is pretty non-committal. Rather than pulling the trigger and making massive changes right away, a conversation is just passing ideas back and forth with others to see how those ideas fit in their brains and with their own personal experiences. Talk about things you're comfortable with and understand. Talk about things that push you a little and make you feel uncomfortable. More than anything, just talk. It's a great first step toward becoming the teacher you want to be.

Start planning. I can't tell you the number of hours I've spent planning and revising the curriculum of the four levels of Spanish I teach. I've also spent innumerable hours charting out the framework for high school swim team practices. In both instances, I created many more plans than I actually used. Staying up past midnight for days in a row during summer vacation, several months before swim season began, planning percentages of endurance swim versus sprint swim for practices in week eleven of the season. Was it a waste? No way. I knew those practice plans like the back of my hand. If I needed to adjust in the midst of the season, I knew why and where to change things.

It's likely that you have a million ideas circulating in your head right now, so start planning. If you're a list maker, make some lists. If you're calendar-minded, chart out some dates. Why do this, especially if there's a good chance you'll deviate from or totally scrap your ideas? Dwight D. Eisenhower said it best: "Plans are nothing. Planning is everything." Your plans will likely never become anything if they don't have legs. Take out a sheet of paper or open a new Google Doc and give your ideas legs. Start planning, even if it isn't pretty or well-organized.

> We have to decide whether we'll let fear make the decisions or if we'll make decisions and take action.

Punch fear in the face. I love the subtitle of Jon Acuff's book, *Start: Punch fear in the face. Escape average. Do work that matters.* Sounds like a fantastic mantra for teachers, especially those who want to ditch the textbook way of teaching. Acuff left a solid, stable day job to become a full-time, social media expert, author, and public speaker. He had plenty of fear he needed to punch in the face. I guarantee the fear will stare you down if you decide to step outside the comfort of the textbook ways of teaching. Change scared me as I first revamped my teaching practices. It still scares me. In the end, we have to decide whether we'll let fear make the decisions or if we'll make decisions and take action.

DITCH it. Remember the DITCH acronym from the introduction? Let's turn it into some questions to help guide you forward:

Different: How is your instruction different than what you have experienced in other classrooms? How is it very much the same? In what areas would you like to see some change?

Innovative: What grabs your attention outside of education? What do you think grabs your students' attention? How can you incorporate those things into your classroom, even if it hasn't been done before? What are some ways you've seen other teachers innovate? How can that inspire what you do?

Tech-laden: What are some ways that technology has improved your life by making it easier or more enjoyable? How can that translate into the classroom? What's a lifeless or cumbersome classroom process or practice that could be rejuvenated with an infusion of technology?

Creative: What types of products do you and/or your students consume a lot? How can the role of consumer be flipped to creator? How do you or your students demonstrate original ideas? How can those translate to the classroom?

Hands-on: What's an area of teaching that's lost its luster or become bland? How could your students use objects, technology, conversation, etc., to re-engage in that area?

At this point, you're really in the same situation as your students. Day after day they get bombarded with information and must try to make sense of it all. You've now been presented with lots of ideas, and now it's up to you to determine what to do with them.

Remember the advice from the previous chapter: Don't try to do it all at once. Pick one or two ideas that really light your fire and pursue them. Starting with any more than that is often overwhelming.

Why act? The textbook answer is that your students are worth it. They're the future. They're the ones on whom you have the most influence and who have greatest potential for change.

That's all true. Your students *are* worth it.

But that's not the only reason to take action.

Here's why you should act: *You* are worth it.

If you've been frustrated, much like I was, you know something's got to give. You don't deserve to be trapped in the same old instruction day in and day out. You were inspired to teach because you wanted to make a difference. Yes, making a difference is messy and complicated.

Do it anyway. Embrace the messy and the complicated. Go out on a limb because that's where the fruit is. Embrace the uncomfortable and discover what's really possible.

Do the things that have been rattling around in your brain as you've been reading this book. Be brave and take the first step, even if you are unsure of the outcome... especially if you're unsure of it!

Go ahead. You know you want to.

Ditch that textbook!

ON THE BLOG:
DOING ENORMOUS, GAME-CHANGING "MOONSHOT THINKING"

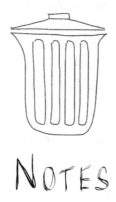

Notes

Chapter 4: Empower Students to Find Their Passions

1 - See the entire study at http://economics.mit.edu/files/9758

2 - http://www.ted.com/talks/ken_robinson_changing_education_paradigms

Chapter 7: Real-World Skills

1 - "futurework—Trends and Challenges for Work in the 21st Century," U.S. Department of Labor Report http://www.dol.gov/oasam/programs/history/herman/reports/futurework/report.htm

Chapter 10: Build Respect and Relationships

1 - http://blogs.kqed.org/mindshift/2012/02/dont-lecture-me-rethinking-how-college-students-learn-2/

Chapter 13: What Every Tech-Using Educator Must Know

1 - Ruben R. Puentedura, Ph.D. is the author of the SAMR model. You can learn more about the model and Puentedura's work at http://hippasus.com/blog and http://tinyurl.com/aswemayteach.

2 - 10 tips to more meaningful Skypes in the classroom: http://ditchthattextbook.com/?s=skype

3 - Source: ECISD Technology: https://sites.google.com/a/ecisd.net/ecisdtech/echs-rocks-with-technology/choose-your-own-adventure/redefining-technology-with-instruction-rti/samr-example---high-school

4 - http://www.apple.com/ibooks-author/

5- Jon Smith classes' ebooks: http://mrsmithtrt.weebly.com/class-ebooks.html

6 - Source: EdofICTJSSALC: http://edofict.wikispaces.com/SAMR+Examples

7 - https://www.thersa.org/discover/videos/rsa-animate/

8 - http://www.schrockguide.net/sketchnoting.html

9 - http://blog.kathyschrock.net/2013/11/sarm-model-musings.html

Chapter 14: Give Students Control

1 - http://www.innovationexcellence.com/blog/2014/08/31/planting-the-seeds-of-innovation-in-education/

Chapter 15: Choose to Cheat

1- http://northpoint.org/messages/breathing-room/choosing-to-cheat

Chapter 16: Minimum Effective Dose

1 - Michael Hyatt's blog post about blogging less: http://michaelhyatt.com/my-new-blogging-frequency.html

Chapter 17: Be a Connected Educator

1 - Get easy instructions at my "Twitter for Teachers" screencast. http://ditchthattextbook.com/2013/03/19/tech-tuesday-screencast-twitter-for-teachers/

Chapter 19: Find What Makes Them Tick

1 - http://www.npr.org/programs/ted-radio-hour/295260995/the-money-paradox

2 - https://www.ted.com/speakers/sir_ken_robinson

3 - http://www.ted.com/talks/dan_pink_on_motivation

Chapter 21: You Are Your Own Best PD

1 - https://www.youtube.com/user/stenhousepublishers/search?query=wormeli

2 - https://www.youtube.com/user/istevideos

3- http://www.spencerideas.org/

4 - https://twitter.com/spencerideas

5 - http://ditchthattextbook.com/2014/01/23/real-change-is-slow-its-discouraging-but-take-heart/

Chapter 22: Sell It to Your Students

1 - Sir Ken Robinson's Keynote Speech to the Music Manifesto State of Play conference on the second day of the event January 17, 2007 http://www.brainhe.com/resources/documents/sir_ken_robinson_musicmanifestoconfkeynote07.pdf

Chapter 23: Create a Home for Your Stuff

1 - http://ditchthattextbook.com/2013/09/26/social-media-duck-dynastys-jase-robertson-and-my-class/

2 - http://ditchthattextbook.com/2013/03/07/6-reasons-why-im-starting-a-teacher-blog-and-why-you-should-too/

Chapter 24: Create Content

1 - http://ditchthattextbook.com/2013/05/07/tech-tuesday-screencast-choose-your-own-adventure-stories/

2- http://ditchthattextbook.com/2015/02/19/15-free-google-drawings-graphic-organizers-and-how-to-make-your-own/

Chapter 25: Write, Read, and Share

1 - http://comments4kids.blogspot.com/

Chapter 26: Go Global

1 - Pernille Ripp's blog: http://pernillesripp.com/2013/08/08/mystery-skype-jobs-created-by-my-students/

Jo-Ann Fox's Mystery Skype Location Call Roles : http://goo.gl/qkv1s5

Chapter 32: Make It Visual

1 - http://en.wikipedia.org/wiki/Picture_superiority_effect

2- Watch a whiteboard video example on my YouTube channel here: https://www.youtube.com/watch?v=tDdJJluOqLU

3 - http://www.digitaltrends.com/computing/best-apps-to-make-animated-gifs/

Chapter 33: Go Where the Kids Are

1 - https://about.twitter.com/company

ALSO FROM
DAVE BURGESS
Consulting, Inc.

TEACH LIKE A *PIRATE*
Increase Student Engagement, Boost Your Creativity, and Transform Your Life as an Educator
By Dave Burgess (@BurgessDave)

Teach Like a PIRATE is the *New York Times'* best-selling book that has sparked a worldwide educational revolution. It is part inspirational manifesto that ignites passion for the profession, and part practical road map filled with dynamic strategies to dramatically increase student engagement. Translated into multiple languages, its message resonates with educators who want to design outrageously creative lessons and transform school into a life-changing experience for students.

P is for PIRATE
Inspirational ABC's for Educators
By Dave and Shelley Burgess (@Burgess_Shelley)

Teaching is an adventure that stretches the imagination and calls for creativity every day! In *P is for Pirate*, husband and wife team Dave and Shelley Burgess encourage and inspire educators to make their classrooms fun and exciting places to learn. Tapping into years of personal experience and drawing on the insights of more than seventy educators, the authors offer a wealth of ideas for making learning and teaching more fulfilling than ever before.

Pure Genius
Building a Culture of Innovation and Taking 20% Time to the Next Level
By Don Wettrick (@DonWettrick)

For far too long, schools have been bastions of boredom, killers of creativity, and way too comfortable with compliance and conformity. In *Pure Genius,* Don Wettrick explains how collaboration—with experts, students, and other educators—can help you create interesting, and even life-changing, opportunities for learning. Wettrick's book inspires and equips educators with a systematic blueprint for teaching innovation in any school.

Learn Like a PIRATE
Empower Your Students to Collaborate, Lead, and Succeed
By Paul Solarz (@PaulSolarz)

Today's job market demands that students be prepared to take responsibility for their lives and careers. We do them a disservice if we teach them how to earn passing grades without equipping them to take charge of their education. In *Learn Like a Pirate*, Paul Solarz explains how to design classroom experiences that encourage students to take risks and explore their passions in a stimulating, motivating, and supportive environment where improvement, rather than grades, is the focus. Discover how student-led classrooms help students thrive and develop into self-directed, confident citizens who are capable of making smart, responsible decisions, all on their own.

Bring the
DITCH THAT TEXTBOOK
message to your school, district, or event!

"Very clear and easy to implement. This is where teaching is heading! We need more of this!"

When you hire Matt Miller to speak, you're putting more than a decade of "in the trenches" teaching experience in the hands of your teachers. He has delivered keynotes, workshops, and concurrent conference sessions to thousands of teachers about technology and its thoughtful integration. He's spoken at International Society for Technology in Education (ISTE), National My Big Campus User Conference, and Google Apps for Education Summits. *Here's what people are saying:*

"Matt's call to 'Ditch That Textbook' couldn't be a timelier message for today's educators and should be an anthem for schools hoping to become more relevant for today's learners. His challenge to replace outdated, traditional practices with more innovative methods is inspiring. Matt leads by example as a practicing teacher, which gives him credibility as he gives his audiences practical ways they can immediately leverage technology to engage their students in authentic and meaningful learning tasks. Teachers will leave a session with Matt motivated to connect with a PLN through social media and eager to improve their practices." —**George Philhower**, Assistant Superintendent, Western Wayne Schools, Pershing, Indiana

"Matt's presentations have been a homerun with our faculty. Whether he is presenting to elementary or secondary teachers, his workshops are dynamic and intensely practical. Matt worked with us to customize training to meet our district's particular needs. His presentations received rave reviews from all teachers and administrators. We were so pleased; we've already asked him back!" —**Susan Drumm**, Instructional Technology Coach, Hamilton Southeastern Schools, Fishers, Indiana

Matt's Popular Presentation Topics Include
Classroom 2.0: 10 Reasons to Go Digital
Connecting Classrooms to the World
Google Genius: Practical Google Activities for Class Tomorrow
A Day in My Paperless Classroom

About the Author

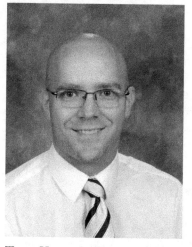

MATT MILLER has been infusing technology and innovative teaching methods into his classroom for more than ten years. After trying to follow traditional practices and "teaching by the textbook" for a few years, he chose to take the less-traveled, textbook-free path. His journey led to technology-inspired, custom learning activities. He and his students like the results—a lot.

Matt's commitment to excellence in teaching and technology integration was recognized by WTHI-TV in Terre Haute, Indiana, with the Golden Apple Award. He was nominated for a Bammy Award for Secondary School Teacher of the Year in 2014. And he has the distinction of being a Google Certified Teacher.

As an author, blogger and education speaker, Matt encourages teachers to free their teaching and revolutionize their classrooms with mindsets, techniques, and curriculum to serve today's learners. With thousands of subscribers and visitors from more than 200 countries, Matt's blog, DitchThatTextbook.com, is a well-respected source of ideas and insights about educational technology and creative teaching.

Before becoming a teacher, Matt was a newspaper reporter and wrote for several Indiana daily newspapers, including the *Indianapolis Star*. He made the switch to education when he realized his true passion wasn't reporting but helping other writers with their writing. He returned to school and started his first teaching job within eight months. The rest is history.

He is a proud graduate of Indiana State University (go Sycamores!) and is living the dream with a wife, three kids, a mortgage, and two dogs.

Connect with him… *he lives for it!*

TWITTER: @jmattmiller
GOOGLE PLUS: plus.google.com/+MattMiller16
YOUTUBE: youtube.com/DitchThatTextbook
PINTEREST: pinterest.com/DitchThatTxt
E-MAIL: matt@DitchThatTextbook.com

CPSIA information can be obtained
at www.ICGtesting.com
Printed in the USA
FSHW01n1216160818
51311FS